Dark Navy

the *Regia Marina* and the Armistice of 8 September 1943

Vincent P. O'Hara and
Enrico Cernuschi

NIMBLE BOOKS LLC

NIMBLE BOOKS LLC

Nimble Books LLC
1521 Martha Avenue
Ann Arbor, MI, USA 48103
http://www.NimbleBooks.com
wfz@nimblebooks.com
+1-734-330-2593

Copyright 2009 by Vincent P. O'Hara and Enrico Cernuschi

Version 1.0; last saved 2009-12-04.

ISBN-13: 978-1-934840-91-7
ISBN-10: 1-934840-91-2

Printed in the United States of America

∞ The paper used in this publication meets the minimum requirements of the American National Standard for Information Sciences—Permanence of Paper for Printed Library Materials, ANSI Z39.48-1992. The paper is acid-free and lignin-free.

Contents

Foreword by Jean Hood iv

Foreword by Erminio Bagnasco v

Preface vii

Chapter 1. Unconditional Surrender? 1

Chapter 2. Seeking the Way Out 5

Chapter 3. The Deal is Done 16

Chapter 4. First Actions 23

Chapter 5. Cast away. 35

Chapter 6. No Safe Havens 42

Chapter 7. A Gentlemen's Agreement. 50

Chapter 8. Defeat through Deception? 58

Chapter 9. On the Knees of the Gods. 65

Appendix I. Operational Italian naval vessels by location as of 8 Sep. 1943 70

Appendix II. German naval vessels in the Mediterranean Sea on 9 Sep. 1943 ... 74

Appendix III. Major Italian Warships Under Repair or still Building on 8 Sep. 1943 75

Appendix IV. The postwar disposition of the Fleet 90

Bibliography 91

NIMBLE BOOKS LLC

FOREWORD BY JEAN HOOD

I was particularly delighted when Vincent O'Hara and Enrico Cernuschi invited me to write the foreword to *Dark Navy* because, put simply, their work has redressed an injustice and, as such, is many years overdue. When Admiral Andrew Cunningham sent the telegram "Be pleased to inform their Lordships that the Italian Battle fleet now lays at anchor under the guns of the fortress of Malta," he wrote no less than the literal truth – but at the same time he created the erroneous but stubbornly persistent impression, underlined by photographic 'evidence,' that the Italian Fleet had either meekly surrendered following the Armistice of 8 September 1943 or been forced to capitulate by the victorious Allies. It is this Anglo-Saxon myth that the authors have comprehensively demolished.

Of the major navies in World War Two, the Regia Marina is arguably the most neglected by historians outside Italy, and few Italian books on the subject have appeared in English translation. I can think of just three, all of them concerned with the exploits of the Decima Flottiglia MAS, the elite special forces unit. When it comes to the Armistice, non-Italian historians tend to hastily brush over this frenetic and frequently bewildering period, seeing it purely from the Allied viewpoint. O'Hara and Cernuschi have unravelled the daunting complexity to produce a lucid account of how, against a background of fast-moving events, negotiations and political intrigue, the Italian Navy obeyed its government's orders to keep its ships out of German hands, and how, when they did indeed lay *at anchor under the guns of the fortress of Malta*, they did not lower their country's flag. *Dark Navy* is a valuable re-assessment of the Italian Navy at a critical moment in World War Two and should be required reading for anyone researching the war in the Mediterranean.

—*Jean Hood*

Books by Jean Hood

Submarine: An Anthology of First-Hand Accounts of the War Under the Sea, 1939-1945 (London: Conway Maritime Press, 2008)

Come Hell and High Water: Extraordinary Stories of Wreck, Terror and Triumph on the Sea (Springfield, NJ: Burford Books, 2007)

Foreword by Erminio Bagnasco

For the Regia Marina (the Royal Italian Navy) the armistice of 8 September 1943 was a very hard test of its personnel's consciences and an ordeal for the fleet's strength---the huge impact of which would be completely appreciated only much later.

Even if the navy saved the main battle force, whose core was still operative after 39 months of war, rallying finally in harbours under Allied control, the armistice and, in a smaller scale, the later co-belligerency, caused serious losses: 356 commissioned warships and auxiliaries and an additional 251 vessels on the slips or fitting out. This totalled more than 500,000 tons displacement, that is, 70 percent of the Italian navy's strength on 10 June 1940 when the war begun, not including 245,000 tons of new construction and seizures commissioned during three years of war.

Many of the losses caused by the armistice crisis were warships of all sizes in northern and mid-Italian yards and harbours for repairs or maintenance and manned by skeleton crews. As a rule they were scuttled, sabotaged or relinquished; the Germans seized them, but the Kriegsmarine armed only a fraction of the minor vessels for its own purposes.

A comparison between the 397 warships and auxiliary vessels displacing 335,000 tons, lost by the Italian navy in all theatres of war from 11 June 1940 to 8 September 1943 and the half million tons mentioned above, most of which were lamented within 24 hours, is a shock, even more so as there was nearly no offset. It was a balance far worse than the most pessimistic forecasts conceived by the few who had decided to ask for and accept the armistice, not to mention the loss of the peninsula's naval bases, depots and logistic infrastructure in the Tyrrhenian Sea and in the upper and middle Adriatic.

In other words the 8 September 1943 armistice was the real disaster which crippled the Regia Marina during the Second World War along with the related transfer of ships as reparations required by the peace treaty signed in Paris in 1947.

The huge tragedy suffered by the Italian navy and nation has been reduced, until today, to a brief mention in the very few books available abroad about the

NIMBLE BOOKS LLC

Regia Marina's war between 1940 and 1945. It is thus quite important that a new essay directed toward English speaking readers is dedicated, at last, to these events, allowing them to sortie beyond the confines of Italian naval historiography--which has long debated these themes--and the scanty circulation abroad of the Italian language.

Erminio Bagnasco
Editor of the monthly magazine
STORIA Militare

Books by Erminio Bagnasco

Submarines of World War Two (London: Arms and Armour, 1977)

Le Navi da guerra italiane 1940-1945, with Enrico Cernuschi (Milan: Ermanno Albertelli, 2004)

In guerra sul mare: Navi e marinai italiani nel secondo conflitto mondiale (Milan: Ermanno Albertelli, 2005)

Le navi da battaglia, classe Littorio (1937-1948), with Augusto De Toro (Milan: Ermanno Albertelli, 2008)

Preface

> Secondly and of equal importance [to the occupation of Italian territory is] the immediate surrender to the Allies of the Italian Fleet, or at least its effective demobilization ... The surrender of the fleet will liberate powerful British naval forces for service in the Indian Ocean against Japan and will be most agreeable to the United States.
>
> —*President Roosevelt to Prime Minister Churchill, July 30, 1943*

On 10 June 1940 Benito Mussolini, the head of Italy's government and armed forces, declared war against Great Britain and France, anticipating a short, easy campaign.

Between June 1940 and December 1940 Italy proceeded to fight a "parallel war" alongside Germany. Mussolini considered this a holding action intended to safeguard his Mediterranean and Balkan sphere of influence until the inevitable victory. During this period, the Duce regarded domestic and political issues just as important as military ones—demonstrated by his dispatch of two hundred aircraft, about a sixth of the total Italian air force, to assist Germany during the Battle of Britain, and by the demobilization of more than 600,000 troops just weeks before Italy attacked Greece with inferior forces.

The parallel war ended with Rome's defeat in its invasion of Greece followed by the rout of the Italian 10th Army in Africa between December 1940 and February 1941. German intervention followed and Berlin's swift conquest of Yugoslavia and Greece in April 1941 dimmed Italian hopes of Balkan hegemony. As the North African campaign evolved into a seesaw struggle, Italy's government slowly realized that the conflict it had entered with such little planning and preparation was, in fact, a fight for its very existence.

Gradually, as 1941 turned into 1942, the Axis gained the upper hand in the Mediterranean, thanks, in large part, to the efforts of the *Regia Marina*. Italy's navy had many tasks, but paramount was the job of controlling the Mediterranean's central basin so that Italy could supply the armies in North Africa and prevent the British from reinforcing Egypt and the Middle East via the Mediterranean Sea.

By the summer of 1942, with an Italo-German army poised to strike Alexandria and Malta strangled by the Axis blockade, Rome was cautiously hopeful about the conflict's progress. As late as 23 October 1942, the day the British attacked El Alamein, Mussolini told Reichsmarshall Herman Göring that he "was optimistic as to the outcome of the war."[1]

However, the beginning of the end came just two weeks later when, on 8 November 1942, Anglo-American armies landed in Morocco and Algeria. The Regia Marina undertook a grim struggle to maintain an Axis bridgehead in Africa, transporting men and supplies across the Sicilian Channel in what became known as the Route of Death. However, Allied air, land and sea power proved overwhelming and the Axis position in Africa collapsed in May 1943. The Allies rapidly exploited this success and on 10 July they invaded Sicily, part of the *madrepatria* itself.

---

[1] F. W. Deakin, *The Brutal Friendship: Mussolini, Hitler and the fall of Italian Fascism* (New York: Harper & Row, 1962), 63.

Figure 1. June 1943. All still seems normal at Gropparello, a small village in the Apennine Mountains: a black shirt, an army officer and some Giovani Italiane, the fascist female youth organization. (Teresa Marconi)

Figure 2. La Spezia 14 June 1943, King Victor Emmanuel and Admiral Bergamini inspecting battleship *Littorio*. (Rivista Marittima)

Chapter 1. Unconditional Surrender?

On 24 January 1943, President Franklin D. Roosevelt and Prime Minister Winston Churchill announced their policy of demanding the unconditional surrender of the Axis nations. The American and British heads of state had debated whether to accept an armistice with Italy instead to entice it out of the war, but the British foreign office protested noting that, "Knowledge of all rough stuff coming to them is surely more likely to have desired effect on Italian morale."[2] Thus, Italy remained grouped with Germany and Japan in this regard; nonetheless, based on contacts between Italian politicians and minor Allied officials in Switzerland, Mussolini received a detailed account of the Casablanca conference and, along with the king, the party, the three services and the nation's financial barons, formed the impression that the principal of unconditional surrender would not apply to Italy.[3]

By the time of the Sicily invasion such distinctions had become important. Mussolini's war policy was clearly bankrupt. The idea of playing the despised junior partner in Germany's final *Götterdämmerung*, and the prospect of waging this battle of annihilation up the length of the Italian peninsula, had little appeal to most of Italy's leadership, especially the military high command.

On 24 July, in an atmosphere of growing crisis, the Fascist Grand Council gathered for the first time since December 1939. This extraordinary meeting was the result of maneuvers undertaken by two sets of plotters, one led by certain council members and the other by General Vittorio Ambrosio, chief of the general staff of Italy's high command, *Comando Supremo,* and his right-hand man, General Giuseppe Castellano. While both factions sought to replace the Duce, the meeting's declared agenda was whether to petition the king, Victor Emmanuel III, to resume the supreme military command he had delegated to Mussolini in June 1940 shortly before war was declared. Mussolini attended and warned the council that a vote to petition would cause "the crisis of the re-

---

[2] Winston Churchill, *The Hinge of Fate* (Boston: Houghton Mifflin Company, 1950), 614. Also see The Casablanca Conference (http://digicoll.library.wisc), 506 and 635.
[3] See Giacomo Acerbo, *Tra due plotoni d'esecuzione* (Bologna, Cappelli Editore, 1968), 483-487 and Alberto Pirelli, *Taccuini 1922/1943* (Bologna: Il Mulino, 1984), 405-425.

gime." Nonetheless, the council so voted to the Duce's amazement (he had been an ill and confused man since late June 1942). Most of those present believed (or so they later claimed) that the Duce's political position was not at issue. They thought that the vote would force the Royal House to openly align itself on the side of fascism and that such a dramatic action by the typically aloof king would energize the nation to throw back the invaders. In fact, the vote presaged royal action, but not in the way many council members expected.

Figure 3. Leghorn Naval Academy, June 1943. The Duce's photo still hangs between the king and queen, but not for long. (Andrea Tani)

The next afternoon Mussolini motored to the royal estate to discuss what actions the council's vote would require. Victor Emmanuel greeted the Duce, dismissed him as premier and had a platoon of *carabinieri* standing by to place him in custody for "his personal protection."

That evening one council member, Giovanni Balella, president of the Industrialist League, saw a clerk chiseling off the fasces (the symbol of Italian fascism, much like the swastika symbolized Germany's national socialism) that decorated the entry to the league's headquarters. He shouted from his office window, "What the hell are you doing?" The worker answered, "Excellency, fascism is over." Balella remembered that he returned to his desk shook his head and said, "That was not what we voted for last night."[4]

---

[4] Egidio Ortona, *Diplomazia in guerra* (Bologna: Il Mulino, 1993).

The king immediately formed a new government under Field Marshal Pietro Badoglio, the 71-year-old conqueror of Abyssinia who had been hovering on the fringes of Italy's power structure since his dismissal as Comando Supremo's chief of staff in November 1940. Although Badoglio proclaimed to his war-weary nation that Italy would fight on, few believed him, least of all the Germans. Six weeks later, on 8 September 1943, Badoglio announced that the Kingdom had agreed to an armistice with the Allies.

The Byzantine intrigues that preceded this armistice, and the chaos that followed, traumatized Italy. However, while the army and air force disintegrated Italy's Regia Marina maintained its discipline, most of its forces, and was the only one of Italy's armed services to effectively fight the Germans.

Dark Navy examines the actions and the role of the Regia Marina during these difficult days in the context of Comando Supremo's failed machinations to exit the war in a neat and bloodless fashion. As is the case with many failures, the facts are complicated by a historiography that is contradictory, self-serving and sometimes mendacious.[5] It rejects the analysis that appears in most English works, epitomized by the official British history's conclusion: "In all the annals of military history there can be few such dramatic events as the submission of an enemy navy. ... For the vanquished it means, by its very completeness, the abandonment of all ambitions. It is the final and irreversible admission of defeat at sea."[6] In fact, the Regia Marina did not surrender, nor did it admit defeat at sea. Although the naval command was excluded from the armistice process, it abided—sometimes grudgingly—by the spirit of the terms Badoglio's government negotiated. This spared the Allies a final showdown with its battle fleet and provided them a useful ally for the balance of the war.

---

[5] In statements made to the Italian commission of inquiry and in subsequent books and interviews, the three principals, Marshal Badoglio, Generals Vittorio Ambrosio and Giuseppe Castellano accused each other of knowing of decisive details (while remaining themselves selectively ignorant of important facts) and of being responsible for the fatal choices. See Ruggero Zangrandi, *L'Italia tradita* (Milan: Mursia, 1971), 403-16.

[6] Stephen Roskill, *The War at Sea Volume III: The Offensive Part 1* (London: HMSO, 1960), 168-69.

Map 1. Italy, 25 July 1943. (Vincent P. O'Hara)

Chapter 2. Seeking the Way Out

The Badoglio government's first diplomatic initiative was to the Germans. On 26 July the king asked the Reich's ambassador in Rome for a meeting with Hitler. The purpose was to propose an armistice with the USSR, a course of action Mussolini himself had vainly recommended since December 1941. The Duce's arrest, however, had enraged the Führer and he was in no mood to treat with the perpetrators of this treacherous act. On 27 July elements of the 2nd Fallschirmjager Division began landing at airports near Rome. The Germans explained that they were on their way to Sicily to join their comrades of the 1st Division, but the troops did not move out and the truth was that they had arrived, as Goebbels' Diary entry for 27 July expressed it, "to occupy Rome, arrest the King with his entire family, as well as Badoglio and his henchmen, and fly them to Germany." The only thing restraining Hitler's mailed fist was uncertainty about Mussolini's whereabouts and fear for his wellbeing.[8]

On the morning of 30 July the Italian Army attaché in Berlin repeated to Hitler himself the proposal for a meeting with the king. The Führer responded with an furious outburst that sent the attaché flying to the telephone where he explained to Rome (in Sardinian dialect, the Italian equivalent of the Navajo language used by the U.S. Marine Corps to guarantee secure communications) that his mission had failed and that German intentions toward the king and the new government were perilously hostile.[9]

That same afternoon Marshal Badoglio and General Ambrosio instructed the new foreign minister, Baron Raffaele Guariglia, to sound out the British and American ministers at the Vatican. Guariglia went to the apostolic palace that night, but the Allied representatives there could do little as they lacked speedy, secure communications. For example, a telegram sent by the chargé at the Vati-

---

[8] Louis P., Lochner, ed. *The Goebbels Diaries 1942-1943* (New York: Doubleday & Company, 1948), 408.

[9] Sergio Pelagalli, "L'8 settembre a Berlino," *Storia Militare*, (April 1994); Jo' di Benigno, *Occasioni mancate* (Rome: S.E.I., 1945).

can on 6 August went by diplomatic pouch to the American Legation at Bern and from there to Washington, where it arrived on 10 September.[10]

Figure 4. General Vittorio Ambrosio, chief of staff of Comando Supremo from February 1943 and one of the principal architects of the armistice fiasco. (Mondadori)

On 31 July Guariglia dispatched emissaries to neutral nations where, beginning on 4 August, they spent two weeks trying to convince British diplomats in Portugal, Tangiers and Switzerland of their bona fides. The British rebuffed these initiatives, characterizing them as " … informal approaches from individuals acting on behalf of Italian generals, [and having] no firm evidence of the readiness of the new Italian Government to negotiate or surrender."[11] In fact, Mussolini's sudden fall from power had caught the Allies without a coherent policy. As Roosevelt expressed it to Churchill on 30 July, "[if the new government seeks to negotiate an armistice], it will be necessary for us to make up our minds first of all upon what we want and secondly upon the measures and conditions

---

[10] United States Department of State, *Foreign relations of the United States. Conferences at Washington and Quebec, 1943*. Substantive Preparatory Papers, *The Chargé at Vatican City* (Tittmann) to the Secretary of State, 569.

[11] F. H. Hinsley, *British Intelligence in the Second World War: Abridged Version* (New York: Cambridge University Press, 1993), 349.

required to gain it for us." The British Foreign Office, on the other hand, knew what it wanted and that was the imposition of harsh political and economical terms designed to punish what it regarded as Italy's unscrupulous opportunism for entering the war in the first place; the British Foreign Secretary, accordingly, instructed his Consul General in Tangiers, who received what the Allies considered the most official of the contacts, that "our position is that we must insist on unconditional surrender before we name our terms."[12] Given Badoglio and Ambrosio's understandable desire for guarantees before they unleashed German retribution, this unbending approach guaranteed the failure of these peace feelers.

Berlin, unlike the Allies, did have a coherent Italian policy. Hitler scheduled the seizure of Rome and the arrest of the king and Badoglio for 2 August. First, an armored regiment of the 26th Panzer Division, in transit to join the rest of the division in southern Italy, halted north of Rome and joined the 3rd Panzergrenadier Division stationed there. The Italians protested to no effect, but worse was coming. On the night of 30/31 July a mountain brigade, hurriedly formed from cadets of an alpine warfare school located in Austria, forced the Brenner Pass—their train crashed the barrier while a company of Tiger tanks moved in to protect their line of communications. Meanwhile, the 305th and 76th infantry divisions—in a previously scheduled movement—arrived at the Franco-Italian border. There the border guards stopped their trains, and likewise repelled an attempt to enter on foot. The situation threatened open conflict until, on the afternoon of 2 August, Ambrosio blinked and ordered the obstacles removed. The next day Wehrmacht troops entered without further incident while elements of the 1st SS Panzer Division Leibstandarte began arriving at the Brenner Pass from Russia.

As troops filtered into northern Italy Hitler gave Otto Skorzeny, commander of his newly formed commando unit, SS Jäger-Bataillon 502, the job of finding and rescuing Mussolini. However, Italian intelligence frustrated his efforts

---

[12] United States Department of State, *Foreign Relations of the United States. Conferences at Washington and Quebec, 1943. Substantive Preparatory Papers, President Roosevelt to Prime Minister Churchill,* July 30, 1943. Also, *The British Foreign Secretary (Eden) to the British Acting Consul General at Tangier (Watkinson),* 576.

to pinpoint the Duce's location with a variety of false leads. These caused the operation's postponement until 4 August and then its cancellation the next day.[13]

During this period, the Italian navy monitored the fleet's security. On 4 August, as German elements were marching towards the main naval bases of La Spezia and Genoa, "to improve the coastal defenses there," Admiral Raffaele De Courten, the chief of staff of *Supermarina*, the navy high command, responded by obtaining the immediate transfer of two army divisions to these ports to forestall a "new Toulon." De Courten, a former attaché in Berlin, the son of a German mother and a proponent of the Axis alliance, was skeptical about the prospects of reaching terms with the Allies. Nonetheless, Supermarina drafted contingency plans to send the battle fleet to La Maddalena in Sardinia, with the king and the government aboard, should hostilities with the Germans actually erupt.[15] General Field Marshal Albert Kesselring paid De Courten a back-handed compliment when he wrote that he was "ostensibly the most accommodating" [of the Italian top commanders] but in the end "the biggest disappointment of the lot."[16]

On 6 August Comando Supremo finally acknowledged that it had misjudged the number of divisions Germany had available to intervene and that northern Italy up to the Pisa-Rimini line through the Apennines Mountains was potentially lost if the Germans attacked. It hurriedly dispatched the first two battalions of the new Ciclone airborne division supported by an artillery regiment equipped with 105/28-mm antitank guns to guard the Apennine passes of Futa, Giogo and Casaglia, which divided northern and central Italy.

There followed a tense meeting between the German and Italian foreign ministers and military commands on 6 August at the Tarvisio Pass. As an American aptly summarized, "The full scope of German intentions—to compel the Italian Government to continue the war whether it wished or not, to seize the Italian Fleet and capital, and to convert the Italian peninsula into a battle-

---

[13] Albert N Garland and Howard McGaw Smyth. *Sicily and the Surrender of Italy* (Washington, D.C.: U.S. Government Printing Office, 1965), 368.
[15] Arturo Catalano Gonzaga, *Per l'onore dei Savoia*, (Milan: Mursia, 1996), 52-54.
[16] Albert Kesselring, *Kesselring: A Soldier's Record* (New York: William Morrow, 1954), 207.

field for the defense of Germany—was abundantly clear after the Tarvisio conference. The German occupation of Italy, which had been Ambrosio's greatest fear since May, was rapidly becoming an accomplished fact." Following the conference Ambrosio hurried to make a deal with the Allies before the Germans could restore Mussolini to power.[17] He sent Badoglio a proposal drafted by General Castellano for direct negotiations between Comando Supremo and the Allied high command, hoping that this would cut through the diplomatic fuss, which so far had failed to bear fruit. Badoglio endorsed the idea, but kept it secret from the cabinet and the king, again in the interests of security. He feared a fascist counter-coup and wanted to maintain deniability should negotiations turn sour.

By 17 August the *Regio Esercito* mustered 2.1 million men within Italy facing less than 500,000 Germans, including eight divisions in Southern Italy, Sardinia and Corsica; however, Italy's forces were scattered and many formations were second-rate. There were twenty-four divisions in France and northern Italy, including five immobile coastal divisions; nineteen (eight coastal) divisions in Central and Southern Italy; eleven (five coastal) in Sardinia and Corsica; eighteen in Yugoslavia and Albania; and eleven in Greece and the Aegean. Many units in Italy were being reconstructed or in training and had no artillery or motor vehicles. Nearly half the troops were in depot, administrative or training units and were poorly armed, if at all. Finally, the border defenses manned by the *Guardia alla Frontiera* lacked the munitions to slow, much less stop a German advance.[18] Although General Antonio Sorice, Italy's minister of war, had recommended the recall of the 4th Army from France and the 2nd Army from Croatia, which would have immensely improved Italy's balance of forces vis-à-vis the Germans, Badoglio demurred, not wishing to provoke a confrontation, with the Allied attitude up in the air.

---

[17] Garland and McGaw Smyth, *Sicily and the Surrender of Italy*, 372. On the German side Ribbentrop allegedly stated that it was clear to him "when Ambrosio and Guariglia presented themselves at Tarvisio, that Italy wanted to abandon Germany". Deakin, *Brutal Friendship*, 510.

[18] Emilio Canevari, *La guerra italiana* (Rome: Tosi, 1949), 592-93.

Figure 5. Baron Raffaele Guariglia and German's foreign minister, Joachim von Ribbentrop, at the 6 August 1943 Tarvisio Pass conference. (Storia Militare)

General Castellano, meanwhile, carried the same instructions given to the previous Italian envoys—to solicit truce terms. He made his way to Lisbon where he met with the British ambassador on 17 August. However, in addition to his instructions, Castellano had his own ideas on the best course of action for Italy to follow. The general surprised the ambassador with the offer of Italian military cooperation against Germany. He repeated this offer to staff officers dispatched from Algiers by General Dwight D. Eisenhower on the 19th. The Allied supreme commander, less than a month away from invading the mainland, endorsed a deal that included Italian military cooperation and the Combined Chiefs of Staff hurriedly prepared a recommendation to the President and Prime Minster that the terms of Italy's unconditional surrender be modified in favor of

Italy depending on the degree of military cooperation provided.[19] After a cordial nine-hour discussion with Eisenhower's officers, Castellano received the "short armistice" terms favored by Allied military headquarters that contained only military conditions and omitted most of the political and economic clauses championed by the British and specified in the so-called "long terms." However, Castellano had no link or codes to communicate with his government and did not leave Lisbon until 23 August to make his leisurely way back to Rome via train finally arriving on the evening of the 27th.

Meanwhile, because Castellano had been gone so long, Rome began to fear that German counterintelligence had seized him, and Badoglio decided to dispatch another envoy, General Giacomo Zanussi, a Castellano rival. He arrived in Lisbon on 26 August and discovered what had transpired with Castellano's mission. The Allies were somewhat disconcerted to have another representative suddenly appear and at first refused to treat with Zanussi. However, on that same day at Quebec, Churchill and Roosevelt finally agreed that Italy would be subjected to the political conditions specified in the "long terms." The British government responded to this development with "extraordinary speed" and delivered the text of the onerous "long terms" to Zanussi even before Eisenhower's headquarters received it. When Eisenhower's staff finally got the document later that day, they became "thoroughly alarmed."[20] Zanussi assumed that Castellano was carrying a copy of these same terms and Eisenhower made sure he did not have a chance to check with his government. On 28 August Zanussi was taken under military hospitality and whisked away to Algiers.

Upon learning of Castellano's initiative upon his return to Rome, Badoglio and Ambrosio decided to stand by the general's offer of collaboration, but to counter-propose that, due to Italian weakness in the face of the German threat, the Allies must land in sufficient force near enough to Rome to guarantee the

---

[19] Giuseppe Castellano, *La guerra continua* (Milan, Rizzoli, 1963), 55-56. Also see "C.C.S 311 Enclosure, Suggested Action on Italian Peace Feelers" Allied Military Conferences 14 Aug 1943 to 24 Aug 1943 (Quebec), footnote.com/image/27511388.

[20] Garland and McGaw Smyth, *Sicily and the Surrender of Italy*, 456.

government's safety and a German withdrawal to the Pisa-Rimini line or, better, the Alps.[21]

The second round of negotiations commenced in Sicily on 31 August. Castellano arrived from Rome with instructions to seek an Allied landing by at least fifteen divisions north of the Italian capital. The Allied negotiators replied that if they could land fifteen divisions north of Rome, they would not be discussing Italian cooperation. They also rebuffed Castellano's attempts to determine the date, strength and location of the Allied operation. They did, however, make one concession; having decided to conduct an amphibious assault south of Naples, they were anxious to reach an accord. In light of the importance of Rome and the relative weakness of the Italian divisions in the area, they agreed to land an airborne division and 100 anti-tank guns near the capital on the day of the invasion.

Castellano presented this offer to Rome on the evening of 31 August. Badoglio had already retired for the night, so Badoglio, Ambrosio, Castellano and General Giacomo Carboni, the commander of the motorized corps around Rome, met the next day. With Italy's situation deteriorating every day, Badoglio and Ambrosio accepted the vague and disingenuous assurances being given to Castellano about the size, timing and location of the forthcoming invasion as meeting their requirements. Although Carboni objected that the Anglo-Americans were not to be trusted and that his troops lacked the munitions and gasoline needed to effectively resist the Germans, the generals finally radioed their acceptance of the Allied terms that afternoon. Castellano flew back to Sicily where he and General Eisenhower's representative signed an armistice on the evening of 3 September. The American general considered the terms "unduly harsh" and felt that Allied governments were looking "to make a propaganda Roman Holiday."[22]

---

[21] Pietro Badoglio, *Italy in the Second World War* (Westport Conn.: Greenwood Press, 1976), 70; Elena Agarossi, *A Nation Collapses: The Italian Surrender of September 1943* (Cambridge: Cambridge University Press, 2000), 76; Garland and McGaw Smyth, *Sicily and the Surrender of Italy*, 466-7.

[22] Dwight Eisenhower, *Crusade in Europe* (Garden City, N.Y.: Doubleday, 1948), 18. The second quote comes from Samuel Eliot Morison, *History of United States Naval Operations in*

Figure 6. The signing of the armistice on 3 September 1943.
General Castellano is dressed in the black suit. (U.S. Army)

World War II. Vol. IX, Sicily–Salerno–Anzio, January 1943–June 1944 (Boston: Little, Brown, 1990), 239. See Howard McGaw Smyth, "The Armistice of Cassibile." *Military Affairs*, 12(1) (Spring 1948): 12-35 for an extensive account of the negotiations.

Figure 7. Castellano shaking hands with General Eisenhower. (U.S. Army)

Map 2. Deployments 8 September 1943. (Vincent P. O'Hara)

Chapter 3. The Deal is Done.

That same evening Badoglio met with the chiefs of staff of the armed forces—Admiral De Courten for the navy, General Mario Roatta for the army and General Renato Sandalli for the air force—and advised them that armistice negotiations were underway. He did not reveal that the deal was already signed and that the terms included cooperation with the Allies. The fact that the government's military leaders and even the king were kept in such ignorance explained much of what followed.[23] Beside their fear of treachery, Badoglio and Ambrosio pinned their extraordinary discretion on the expectation that the Germans would, when faced by a massive Allied landing around Rome, retreat to the north; even better they hoped the German army or the SS would depose Hitler and propel the Reich into a replay of the 1918 collapse. Such a scenario would result in the forgiveness of all sins and make heroes of the two generals.[24]

Badoglio, despite later protestations that the British and Americans kept him in the dark, knew by 5 September the broad outline—if not the exact de-

---

[23] The role of King Victor Emmanuel and his knowledge of these proceedings is much debated. Five years after the king's death Badoglio wrote that he received Victor Emmanuel's approval ("I went immediately to see the King to receive his orders and then informed Ambrosio that the armistice was to be accepted." Badoglio, *Italy at War*, 71.) However, other evidence indicates that only on the afternoon of 8 September did the Marshal tell the king that he had signed a full armistice and not a truce, which would have allowed the Germans to retire safely home. Moreover, the crown council of 8 September debated Ambrosio's idea—devised the day before—of deposing Badoglio in favor of Marshal Caviglia, because the instrument confirming General Castellano's powers contained only Badoglio's signature. See, Raffaele de Courten, *Le memorie dell'ammiraglio De Courten* (Rome: Ufficio Storico della Marina Militare 1993), 207-228; Paolo Sandalli, *8 settembre 1943: forze armate e disfattismo* (Rome: Gruppo Editoriale Gesualdi, 1993), 30-41; Raffaele Guariglia, *Memorie* (Naples: Scientifiche Italiane, 1950), 704-711; Paolo Monelli, *Roma 1943*, (Milan: Longanesi, 1963), 310-12; Paolo Puntoni, *Parla Vittorio Emanuele III* (Milan: Palazzi, 1958), 161-64; Matteo Mureddu, *Il Quirinale del Re* (Milan: Feltrinelli, Milan, 1977), 119-121; Giuseppe Bucciante, *I generali della dittatura*, (Milan: Mondadori, 1987), 538; Giacomo Zanussi, *Guerra e catastrofe d'Italia* (Rome: Corso, 1946), 180-83.

[24] For the general expectation of a sudden German collapse on August 1943 see Richard Lamb, *The Ghosts of Peace 1935-1945* (Wilton, Salisbury: Michael Russel Publishing, LTD, 1987), 314-15. Joachim Fest, *Staatsstreich, Der lange Weg zum 20 Juli* (Berlin, Wolf Jobst Siedler Verlag. GmbH, 1994), chapter 7; Alberto Pirelli, *Taccuini 1922/1943* (Bologna: Il Mulino, 1984), 429; Giuseppe Pardini, "Le ultime ore del PNF, il processo Scorza", *Nuova Storia Contemporanea* (6/2001); Enzo Galbiati, *Il 25 luglio e la MVSN* (Milan: Bernabò, 1950); Roberto Festorazzi, *Farinacci, l'antiduce* (Rome: Il Minotauro, 2004), 303-5; Luigi Bolla, *Perchè a Salò* (Milan: Bompiani, 1982), 96-102.

tails—of the Allied invasion plan, which Eisenhower modified in expectation of Castellano's promised support. On 6 September the Marshal informed General Roatta that an armistice had been decided and that after its announcement the Allies would land near Rome with six divisions and that a U.S. paratroop division would descend on the capital's airports and an armor division at the mouth of the Tiber River. However, he kept the navy and air force in the dark, only warning them that day that there was a danger of a German coup against the government.[25]

The navy had fought a long and bitter war against the British. It had suffered several large defeats, like the air raid against Taranto and the ambush of a cruiser division at Matapan, but it also had some brilliant successes and had fulfilled its major missions. At this juncture, with Sicily lost, there was sentiment for leaving the war, but it was hardly universal. Admiral De Courten was skeptical that the armistice discussions would bear fruit. Cruiser divisions continued to raid south and the outnumbered, but still powerful battle fleet prepared to contest an Allied landing on the mainland. It had not intervened in the Sicilian fighting because of the lack of air support and the prohibitive odds it faced with only *Littorio* and *Vittorio Veneto* available against six British battleships and two fleet carriers. But these conditions did not pertain to an invasion of the mainland. "Consequently the principal element in the Navy's planning was that it would fight out this last phase to the finish, utilizing all of its remaining fighting forces, from battleships to torpedo boats" regardless of odds.[26] There was no political alternative.

On 7 September, as De Courten planned the fleet's last stand, an Italian corvette, secretly dispatched by Supermarina following an order from Ambrosio to exchange at sea some experts to discuss the military terms of the pending armistice, brought two mysterious passengers to the capital. They were General Maxwell Taylor deputy commander of the U.S. 82nd Airborne Division, and an USAAF colonel. They arrived ostensibly to inspect the airfields that would re-

---

[25] Giuseppe Fioravanzo, *La Marina dall'8 settembre 1943 alla fine del conflitto*, (Rome, Ufficio Storico della Marina Militare, 1971), 15-21.
[26] Marc' Antonio Bragadin,. *The Italian Navy in World War II* (Annapolis: Naval Institute, 1957), 307-8.

ceive Taylor's division, but also to verify Italian support. Their reception instead inspired doubt.

Ambrosio had disappeared on a railroad trip to his home in Turin purportedly "to pick up his diary and other compromising documents," but in fact, to engineer a last minute shuffle in the shell game he was playing with his nation and government. The general's few subordinates aware of the armistice (a total of five officers and NCOs) had contacted him that afternoon with shocking news. Air reconnaissance had confirmed an Allied amphibious armada gathering in the waters around Palermo; the invasion was expected to materialize within two days, and the destination seemed to be southern Italy or Sardinia. Ambrosio had anticipated a landing near Rome on 12 September. A landing south of Naples, however, would allow the Germans to seize the capital and fight a slow rearguard action in front of the Allies, frustrating all his plans.[27]

In the face of this shocking news Ambrosio quickly conceived a counterstroke. He prepared to replace Badoglio with the respected and pro-German Marshal Enrico Caviglia, one of Badoglio's long-standing rivals, and to persuade the king to continue the pro-Axis policy. On that evening of 7 September Ambrosio stopped his personal train in Liguria, roused the Marshal from his house, and brought him to Rome, where he planned a royal audience on the morning of 9 September. As a matter of fact an Allied assessment of Italian leadership, written in October 1942, thought more of Caviglia than Badoglio, noting that, "Marshal Caviglia comes nearest to measuring up to the job [of being Italy's future leader], but he is nearly eighty years old. Marshal Badoglio has the reputation of being too much out for himself to be a popular leader. He might, however, prove an adequate chief during the transition period after the fall of the present regime. He has the confidence of the Royal Family and the Army."[28]

While Ambrosio was seeking another figurehead, General Carboni received Taylor. Carboni still doubted Allied intentions and claimed his troops were incapable of effectively supporting an Allied airborne landing, but most of all he was shocked that the landings would be occurring in less than 24 hours. He pro-

---

[27] Garland and McGaw Smyth, *Sicily and the Surrender of Italy*, 494.
[28] Pier Paolo Cervone, *Caviglia, l'anti Badoglio* (Milan: Mursia, 1997), 239. See http://www.fdrlibrary.marist.edu/psf/box52/a468g12.html for the assessment of Caviglia

tested to Taylor that the armistice must be delayed. The American general found his pessimism alarming and insisted on seeing Badoglio. Taylor wrote, "It was not easy to arrange a meeting on such short notice with an aged soldier-politician who did not like being disturbed in the middle of the night during an air alert. Nevertheless our call was arranged by telephone and we groped our way in Carboni's car across blacked-out Rome through sentry check points and finally reached Badoglio's villa on the edge of town around midnight. ... Badoglio received us cordially, if informally, in his pajamas." Taylor verified that Badoglio wanted the armistice announcement postponed and had him put it in writing to Eisenhower. He also cancelled the parachute operation, the news arriving at the airfield after some aircraft were already in the air. The next day Eisenhower curtly telegrammed Badoglio that he would make the announcement as agreed and threatened, "That if I did so without simultaneous action on his part Italy would have no friend left in the war."[29]

Supermarina's original plan to contest an invasion of the Italian mainland called for the main battle squadron—based at La Spezia and Genoa, and which included three modern battleships, five cruisers and eight destroyers—to sortie from its northern Italian harbors after dark. Come dawn German and Italian aircraft would provide cover, taking advantage of newly developed ship-to-air radio links, and the squadron would arrive in the battle zone late that morning. De Courten left a brief meeting with Ambrosio on the morning of 8 September with the impression that the peace initiative had failed, and he ordered the battle fleet to raise steam early and sail that same day for Salerno. Such an act would have compromised the air cover in the north Tyrrhenian Sea, but it would also have eliminated the doubts of the previous days and confirmed Italy's place by Germany's side. However, at 1430 Comando Supremo phoned, "Do not, repeat, do not sortie." The battleships continued raising steam nonetheless, grouping to sail with the cover of darkness according to the original plan.[30]

---

[29] See the account in Garland and McGaw Smyth, *Sicily and the Surrender of Italy*, 500-501. The first quote is from Maxwell D. Taylor, *Swords and Plowshares* (Cambridge, Mass.: Da Capo, 1990), 58. The second quote is from Eisenhower *Crusade in Europe*, 186.

[30] Andrea Amici, *Un pomeriggio di settembre* (Genoa: De Ferrari, 2006), 89-93. Amici was an NCO aboard the battleship *Roma* and he saved the record of engine room orders made that day.

On 8 September shortly before 1700, an embarrassed Badoglio, with Eisenhower's curt reply in hand, and after a troublesome encounter with Ambrosio, advised King Victor Emmanuel that the American general would make a radio declaration that evening announcing an armistice with Italy. King Victor, astonished by this news, immediately summoned a crown council to consider Italy's next move. When they arrived Admiral De Courten and the air forces' General Sandalli were shocked and both vigorously recommended denouncement. After collecting opinions, the king briefly considered the matter and then announced that he would confirm the actions of Marshal Badoglio and General Ambrosio.[31] He had run out of time in any case. Badoglio's pleas for a deferred proclamation had induced Eisenhower to suspect an about-face so he advanced his broadcast originally scheduled for later that night. At 1830 the Allied supreme commander announced that the Italian government had surrendered its armed forces unconditionally and that, "All Italians who now act to help eject the German aggressor from Italian soil will have the assistance and the support of the United Nations."[32]

Bypassed by events, Marshal Badoglio reluctantly went on Radio Rome and proclaimed at 1947: "The Italian Government ... has requested an armistice from General Eisenhower. ... This request has been granted. The Italian forces will therefore cease all acts of hostility against the Anglo-American forces wherever they may be met. They will, however, oppose attack from any other quarter."[33]

Immediately after the crown council and before Badoglio's broadcast De Courten and Sandalli issued orders stopping the battle fleet and the first wave of torpedo bombers. When Supermarina's orders arrived at 1945 only the battleship *Vittorio Veneto* was still at her buoy ready to join her sister ships in the roads and set course for Salerno. However, the two chiefs of staff refused to apply Allied conditions that required the fleet to sail for Bone and other harbors in Allied possession, and the transfer of the planes to Sicily and Tunisia, because such requirements seemed unnecessary and dishonorable.

---

[31] De Courten, *Le Memorie*, 212.
[32] Italian Surrender Documents. http://www.geocities.com/iturks/html/ documents_11.html.
[33] Ibid.

Figure 8. Admiral Carlo Bergamini, the commander of the Italian battle fleet since April 1943. He was lost when *Roma* sank. (Rivista Marittima)

Figure 9. Admiral Luigi Sansonetti, deputy chief of staff of the Italian Navy. (Rivista Marittima)

Upon receipt of the unexpected news of an armistice, Admiral Carlo Bergamini, the battle force's commander, hastily gathered his officers. The majority wanted to scuttle the fleet. But in a series of thundering phone calls that lasted until 2300 De Courten finally convinced Bergamini that the ships had to sail for La Maddalena. General Sandalli, on the other hand, waited until 0600 on 9 September before he ordered the air force to transfer its planes to Sardinia and the

Puglie, and this proved too late. Even if the bases were still available (the Germans did not seize them until the following days), news of the armistice had destroyed morale, already crippled by Mussolini's fall, and the majority of this most fascistic of the armed services rejected the idea of an armistice. On 7 September the *Regia Aeronautica* had 1,289 aircraft, 665 of them in service; 245 obeyed Sandalli's order, of which the Germans shot down about forty joining approximately a hundred already in the south; about two dozen aircraft flew north to join their old ally, forming the nucleus of the Italian RSI (*Repubblica Sociale Italiana*) fascist air force that fought alongside the Germans for the rest of the war.[34]

---

[34] Between August to September 1943 the Italian Air Force's combat readiness had dropped suddenly on all fronts, from the usual 66 percent during the 1940-1943 period to 50 percent. The Regia Aeronautica could deploy 130 serviceable modern fighters. See Gregory Alegi, "L'ala infranta," *Storia Militare*, (January, 2002). Also Achille Vigna, *Aeronautica italiana, dieci anni di storia: 1943-1952* (Parma: Albertelli, 1997).

Chapter 4. First Actions

From Nice in France to Rhodes in the Aegean, clashes between Italian and German troops erupted hard on the heels of the armistice broadcasts. The mingling of Italian and German forces throughout the Mediterranean and Balkans, and the fact that many Italians supported the alliance with Germany, complicated the situation. As a result there was little pattern to the way events played out with some incidents more violent than others, depending on the location and the commands involved.

Figure 10. Rome, 10 September. Street fighting between German and Italian forces. (Storia Militare)

In Bastia, German and Italian warships were docked side-by-side and German troops manned defenses alongside Italian troops. A sailor aboard the torpedo boat *Aliseo*, which had arrived that day as part of the escort for a fast merchant ship, *Humanitas*, remembered hearing about the armistice. "Our ships passed a normal morning. In the afternoon men were granted shore leave. Towards 1800 hours the news that the armistice had occurred hit us like lighting … We were astounded."[35] A German soldier detached from the 16th SS

---

[35] Mario Cardea, "La Brillante Azione Della Torpediniera Aliseo." *Mare – L'Italia Marinara* (September 1952): 2.

Reichführer Brigade was in Bastia and he remembered, "The town was full of drunken Corsicans and Italians, some of them armed and looking for Vichy French soldiers to kill. In the town square the people started to sing the *Marseillaise* along with the *Internationale*, the flags of the Allies along with many communist banners were hoisted. Anti-German graffiti appeared on every wall. The situation was tenuous."[36]

Figure 11. MFPs entering Bastia harbor. (Storia Militare)

That night the SS Brigade seized the town of Bonifacio on Corsica's southern tip and Kriegsmarine forces attacked Portoferraio, the chief city of Elba and the Tuscan port of Piombino.

At Piombino, six armed *Marinefährprahm* (MFP) landing barges loaded with four hundred troops arrived on 8 September, joining four barges already in port. After Badoglio's announcement the navy's port commander contacted the Germans and secured their promise to sail at dawn on the 9th. Instead, German sailors disembarked after dark, disarmed Italian patrols and occupied a coastal battery near the harbor. An Italian machine gun unit engaged the German boats and a navy-manned shore battery of 3-in guns joined in. In fifteen minutes the

---

[36] Vincent P. O'Hara, "Attack and Sink." *World War II* (March 2004): 45.

Italians sank two barges and severely damaged a third. Outgunned and surprised by the violent reaction, the German sailors released their prisoners and retreated to their boats, claiming that the whole affair was a case of mistaken orders.

In fact, the Germans were attempting to secure the chain of harbors necessary to withdraw the 90th Division and the 16th SS Brigade from Sardinia and Corsica. Piombino was at one end of the chain and Bastia a critical link. About five hours after Badoglio's broadcast, the rapid, popping sound of heavy machineguns broke the calm that had, until then, held in the Corsican port.

Aliseo, following orders to continue her mission, had slipped her mooring and was making for the narrow passage between the jetties that enclosed Bastia's outer harbor. *Ardito*, her sister ship, was preparing to get underway when the German subchasers *UJ2203* and *UJ2219*, as well as German manned antiaircraft guns aboard *Humanitas* opened fire on her. A passenger aboard the merchantman recalled:

"At 2330 the silence of the night was disrupted by a loud whistle which was their signal to attack. This woke me. Simultaneously all the ships anchored in port were attacked. The lookouts, one by one, were stabbed or killed with hand grenades and for an hour we stood in danger of suffering the same fate. All of the guns aboard were concentrated on us and we had no choice but to throw ourselves on the ground. … In the stern hold a fire broke out … some of the motor vehicles fell prey to the flames and their fuel tanks as well as a lot of gasoline drums exploded into the air. The fire also threatened the other holds which were loaded with explosives. … On my hands and knees I crawled towards the ladder that was crowded with terrified, panicked soldiers."[37]

The gunfire slaughtered seventy men from *Adito*'s crew of 180. Then sailors from the subchasers and barges stormed the stricken warship while *Aliseo* escaped and stood offshore to await developments.

A similar act played out north of Naples at Gaeta, but with different results. The corvette *Gabbiano* was docked at the small port's outer jetty. Her crew was shocked and amazed by the armistice broadcast. At 0200 on 9 September a pair

---

[37] Alberto Lovatto, "In Corsica dopo l'8 di settembre, Il Diario di Giovanni Milanetti," *L'impegno* (1996).

of German army officers appeared and politely asked to speak to the corvette's commander. One crewman remembered, "Behind them we saw within a few minutes that more soldiers were coming and as soon there were enough men on the mole to match our crew the smiles disappeared and the senior of the two officers asked our commander to rally to the Wehrmacht. To underscore this quite direct proposal he gestured to the troops which were in line on the mole behind him, their weapons at hand." The Italian commander replied he had to speak with the squadron leader who was on the other side of the bay. As soon as he stepped ashore, however, the Germans seized him and soldiers pushed aboard via the stern gangplank. The Italian crew concentrated on the ship's forward sections. Continuing with the crewman's account, "tension was at the utmost. What saved us was the fact the captain had ordered from the first moment to ready for departure by opening a link in the anchor chain. The boatswain and helmsman stood ready and the Germans did not understand that the sensible vibrations of our diesel engines signified that they were finally warmed up after only a quarter hour starting when the first Germans had appeared."

Gabbiano's captain shouted to go. The chain splashed into the water. The corvette leapt away from the dock at full speed tearing free the light mooring cables and rope. The gangplank collapsed spilling German troops into the bay. Others, stunned by the sudden event, jumped or were pushed over the side by Italian sailors. Two machine guns in the pier opened fire and they wounded three men before a 20-mm burst from *Gabbiano* silenced them.

Following orders from Supermarina *Gabbiano* sailed north toward Montecristo Island, joining there her sister ships of the 1st Squadron, *Pellicano* and *Gru*. "No one mentioned Bone or Malta. After eleven months at war we were the record holders among the corvettes with 1,548 hours at sea covering 14,384 miles and had sunk the British submarine *Sahib* on 24 April 1943 rescuing her crew. Surrender be damned! We had just begun to fight in the opposite direction and on 11 and 13 September we took on German bombers and four Kriegsmarine landing craft. We then went to Palermo on 14 September, where the Americans welcomed us in a very sympathetic way."[38]

At Piraeus, the major Grecian base, the Italian destroyers and torpedo boats *Turbine*, *Crispi*, *Calatafimi* and *San Martino* and the auxiliary cruiser *Morosini* were dispersed, according to custom, to present a more difficult target in case of enemy air raids. When the news of the armistice came over the radio *Turbine*'s sailors were jubilant. "Down below, it was a mess. The men crowded around the NCO's commercial radio, which was repeating in every known language the armistice news. Wild rumors were flying. The most common one said we would leave for Brindisi and the crews of two small Italians yard tugs asked to sail with us." As the executive officer (the captain was attending a meeting ashore) ordered the ship to raise steam crewmen observed the German minelayer *Drache* getting underway, deck loaded with dark mines.

At 2100 the captain returned, pleased to see steam was being raised without his orders. The telephone link, however, had been cut and radio signals with the other units of the squadron were being jammed. *Turbine* stood into the fairway and manned all weapons as nervousness replaced the crew's earlier jubilation. Then, a few minutes after midnight, a German car came screeching onto the mole and a German officer ran out waving a white handkerchief. The ship fixed a small searchlight on him revealing *Drache*'s well-known captain, who had sailed beside *Turbine* on many missions. A whaler brought him aboard. The crewman's account continued: "Our commander and the German captain conferred alone on the stern. After some minutes the meeting ended and the Germans were ferried back to the mole. Our commander explained the situation: the German batteries up on the hills surrounding the bay had us in their sights. [*Drache*] had just laid a new minefield, whose position we did not know, of course. At the narrow mouth of the harbor German 150-mm batteries were ready. If we got underway and were so lucky as to avoid all these menaces, the next morning we would be in any case under the coverage of the Luftwaffe base at Tatoi [Athens airport] less than ten minutes flight time away." At dawn the

---

[38] The quotes are taken from Vincenzo Baldieri, "L'avventura della corvetta *Gabbiano*," *Mare – L'Italia Marinara* (October 1952): 3-5. Also see Franco Bargoni, *Esploratori, fregate, corvette e avvisi italiani*, (Rome: Ufficio Storico della Marina Militare, Rome, 1974), 500.

Italian sailors could easily verify the German threat. The crew prepared to scuttle while the captain went ashore. At 1000 instructions came to cool the boilers. At 1120 the captain returned and advised that the Italian Army command in Greece had ordered the ship delivered to the Kriegsmarine intact. In return the Germans promised the crews safe passage to Italy. Some volunteered to serve with the Germans, but most elected repatriation. This unfortunate group, however, was shipped to camps in Germany and Poland.[39]

Figure 12. German troops taking possession of the destroyer *Turbine* at Piraeus on 9 September 1943. (Storia Militare)

At the main naval bases in La Spezia and Genoa there was never any question of surrendering ships or accepting army orders. By 0300 the fleet's battleships, cruisers and destroyers were underway, and once they were safely at sea

---

[39] Luigi Pizzarni, "Una lunga notte di angosciosa attesa" in *L'epopea dei convogli italiani nel Mediterraneo* (Rapallo: Testimonianze, 1987), 113-120.

Supermarina ordered naval facilities in northern Italy to deactivate ships and emplacements for fifteen days, confirming that the optimistic fantasy of a swift German retreat north of the Alpine passes pervaded the thinking in Italy's higher echelons.[40]

Figure 13. Morning 9 September, *Roma, Italia* and *Vittorio Veneto* off Cape Corse steaming south. (Erminio Bagnasco)

Around Rome the gunfire started at 2000 on 8 September. The king, prime minister and military chiefs gathered at the war ministry. Ever since the unexpected appearance of German forces at the Brenner Pass five weeks before, General Ambrosio had calculated he might need to flee the capital with the king if the Germans attempted a putsch. He had two escape plans ready to implement: one to Sardinia though Civitavecchia, and the other to the Pescara airfield on the peninsula's east coast. At about 0330 on 9 September Ambrosio decided it was time for what he hoped would be a temporary exit from Rome.[41] Badoglio was awoken at 0400 to have the situation described to him "in the gloomiest of terms." The prime minister later wrote that the decision to flee the capital was his alone and that his only objective was to maintain contact with the Allies so as to prevent the Germans from establishing a new government that would repudiate the armistice.[42] The king insisted that the military ministers join him at

---

[40] Gino Galuppini, "L'Arsenale di La Spezia nel centenario della sua inaugurazione," *Rivista Marittima* (July 1969).

[41] Mimmo Franzinelli, *Guerra di spie* (Milan: Mondadori, 2004). The appendix contains the diaries of Badoglio's personal pilot.

[42] Badoglio, *Italy at War*, 83-4.

Pescara while the civilian ministers remained in Rome under the leadership of their senior, Umberto Ricci.[43]

As the king and his top generals departed Rome in a car caravan, along a route carefully plotted to avoid German concentrations, Italian soldiers gathered on the outskirts of Bastia. Supported by armored cars, these troops counterattacked at dawn. Their superior fire power routed the German sailors and forced the two Kriegsmarine submarine chasers and the MFPs *F366*, *F387*, *F459*, *F612* and *F623*, along with a 43-ton Luftwaffe motorboat, *FL B.412*, to flee the narrow harbor. As the Germans got underway the Italian port commander radioed *Aliseo*, still standing offshore, and ordered her to attack and sink the German flotilla.

As *Aliseo* turned to engage, *UJ2203* opened fire followed by other German units as they emerged from the port. *Aliseo* replied at 0706 when she was about nine thousand yards from the enemy column. A running fight developed until 0730 when an 88-mm shell struck the torpedo boat's engine room and brought her to a halt. Her crew rapidly repaired the damage and *Aliseo* overhauled the enemy column. She steered to close range and a flurry of 100-mm shells blasted *UJ2203*. At 0820 *UJ2203* exploded, sending an enormous column of smoke into the air. *Aliseo* shifted fire to *UJ2219* and ten minutes later a salvo detonated the second subchaser's magazine. The torpedo boat then targeted the barges and within five minutes she had dispatched three of them. At that point the corvette *Cormorano* arrived and joined the fray. Together the Italian warships drove the last two barges ashore and sank the Luftwaffe motorboat.

Aliseo rescued twenty-five German survivors. She then made course for La Spezia until ordered instead to Portoferraio, reaching that port at 1758.[44]

While *Alieso* was destroying a German flotilla, German anti-aircraft artillery occupying the hills above Genoa sank the minelayer *Pelagosa* as she had left the harbor. At Castellamare di Stabia in the Gulf of Naples, the uncompleted light cruiser *Giulio Germanico*, which could not sail but could work her guns, drove off German troops trying to enter the town.

---

[43] Monelli, *Roma 1943*, 340.
[44] See O'Hara, "Attack and Sink."

Figure 14. Morning of 9 September. The explosion of *UJ2203* off Bastia after being hit by *Aliseo*. (Rivista Marittima)

As dawn broke over Civitavecchia German tanks rumbled into the harbor area. The Italian army troops stationed there, a small-gun army battery, did not offer resistance, and the Germans seized three auxiliary subchasers. One of them (*AS86*) tried to scuttle, but the Wehrmacht soldiers easily stopped the flooding. At 0700 the Italian submarine *Alagi*, which could not dive due to a defect in her flooding system, arrived off the harbor hoping to make repairs. Three German S-boats confronted the sub and escorted her to the mole. The Germans falsely accused *Alagi* of torpedoing and sinking a German warship the night before. Being unable to operate the boat, they demanded that the submarine sail that afternoon with her torpedo pistols removed and her surface weapons neutralized, under the escort of *TA9* and *TA11*, the heaviest German naval units in the western Mediterranean, and the armed freighter *Carbet*. Once they arrived at La Spezia the crew would be allowed to go home. The Italian captain accepted these terms. The boat got underway, but at sunset he suddenly ordered crash dive, without even warning his crew. The defect had, in fact, been repaired on board, but not tested. The well-trained crew obeyed automatically and the boat was able to submerge, avoiding by just a few yards the bow of the torpedo boat behind her. *Alagi* escaped the German depth charges that followed and, after receiving new orders from Supermarina, proceeded to Bone.[45]

In Trieste some officers at the navy barracks wanted to continue fighting alongside the Germans. Soon after midnight rumors that German troops were marching toward the city prompted orders to board the battleship *Cavour* which was repairing in the yard. These were cancelled and renewed two times during the confusing night. The navy command wanted to concentrate men to support the few coastal battalions defending the town. On the battleship, too, sentiments were divided. In the meanwhile motorized Luftwaffe batteries moved into the Opicina hills dominating the harbor. At 0730 on 9 September the corvette *Berenice*, completed a week before and the largest operational warship at Trieste, cast off as soon as the threat from the batteries became apparent, but it was too late. A storm of machinegun fire from German half-track mounted, 20-mm weapons positioned less than 2,000 meters from the ship ripped into *Berenice* as she separated from the pier. Her weapons replied, but within seconds the flak guns had riddled her and she sank forty minutes later.

That afternoon Germans troops entered Trieste, after signing an agreement with the local army command "to defend the town from the threat of a British landing supported by Slav partisans." The Regia Marina command and personnel remained isolated on *Cavour* until the next evening when they left with the battleship's flag. In contrast to the fate of the men at Piraeus, everyone was allowed to go home.[46]

The Allies, naturally, were focused on their invasion of Salerno and had no appreciation for the dramas occurring in every harbor in Italy. What attention they had for the Regia Marina was concentrated on the battle fleet. They learned from air reconnaissance and later from signal intelligence that these ships were not bound for Bone as expected, and that they were not showing the identifications marks (a black pennant and black rounds on the deck) prescribed

---

[45] Marino la Nasa, "Il pomeriggio in cui l'*Alagi* sfuggì ai tedeschi dopo la cattura," *Aria alla rapida*, (15), 27-28.

[46] See Angelo Mangiocavallo, "Una giornata da non dimenticare", *Supplement of the Rivista Marittima* (January, 2004), 49-51 and Franco Bargoni and Franco Gay, *Corazzate classe Conte di Cavour* (Rome: Bizzarri, 1972), 58.

in the armistice instructions. They did not protest, however, being content so long as the Italian battleships did not appear as enemies off Salerno, as the landing there had encountered unexpectedly stubborn German opposition.

Figure 15. The corvette *Berenice* sank at Trieste after being riddled with 20-mm shells. Here she is in 1951 shortly after being raised. (Aldo Fraccaroli)

Map 3. Naval actions September 1943. (Vincent P. O'Hara)

CHAPTER 5. CAST AWAY.

Just after dawn on 9 September the air force's General Sandalli headed for the War Ministry to learn what was happening, as no one had answered his phone calls. He later wrote, "I found General Ambrosio who was very surprised to encounter me and who gave me the order, by his Majesty's will, to leave at once for Pescara airfield. The Premier, the King and the government had already departed Rome and were on their way there. I was shocked." Ambrosio supplied Sandalli with printed, up-to-date maps indicating the safe route out of the city, showing that the chief of staff was well prepared for the government's exodus.[47] However, while the king's will commanded navy and air force compliance, General Sorice, the army minister, who had refused to support the armistice during the crown council meeting on 8 September, declined to join the flight, marking the first fracture in the chain of command.

At 0900 Marshal Caviglia, who was supposed to see the king that morning, arrived at the Quirinal Palace to "find only the doormen on duty—no guards, no carabinieri."[48] Nor could he find a single general officer at Comando Supremo. The government's civilian ministers gathered later that morning, with Caviglia looking on, and learned, to their dismay, that the king, the premier and most of the military leadership had fled. The Minister of the Interior, Ricci, then refused to take charge as he, like the others, had not been informed about the negotiations or about the armistice itself. This duty devolved unto the unhappy foreign minister, Baron Guariglia, who was enraged by the way the armistice had been handled. Caviglia, based on his prestige as a Marshal of Italy, assumed military command of the capital. After Caviglia donned his old uniform and presented himself at the Ministry of War, he quickly learned that, despite Badoglio's later assertions that "everything possible [to defend Rome] had been done," the capi-

---

[47] Sandalli, *8 settembre 1943*, 43-45.
[48] Garland and McGaw Smyth, *Sicily and the Surrender of Italy*, 527-8. Caviglia was a die-hard republican and politics may color his description. Mureddu, *Il Quirinale del Re*, 123 asserts the *carabinieri* remained on duty until 12 September.

tal's defenses were bluff and that the city had only three days of food. Caviglia concluded that a local truce with the Germans was unavoidable.[49]

Grand Admiral Thaon di Revel, the navy's chief of staff during World War One and now president of the senate, quickly endorsed Caviglia's decision. The old Marshal also issued a secret order to the Gran Sasso Hotel where Mussolini was being held that, despite Badoglio's instructions to shoot the ex-Duce if there was the slightest danger the Germans could seize him, he was not to be harmed under any circumstances.[50]

At 1030 a composite force (soon nicknamed *La squadretta*, or little fleet) formed by torpedo boats and corvettes, under the orders of Admiral Amedeo Nomis di Pollone, slipped out of La Spezia for La Maddalena while Admiral Giotto Maranghini, the base commander, negotiated a ceasefire with the Wehrmacht minutes before German troops arrived at the harbor gates. Following orders issued by the king on 7 September, Admiral Nomis forcibly embarked Admiral Aimone, Duke of Aosta, as Victor Emmanuel feared the duke's participation in a German sponsored coup. Another royal admiral, the Duke of Ancona, was bundled onto a floatplane at Venice on 11 September and rushed south for the same reason.

That afternoon, by now knowing what was happening throughout Italy, Maranghini, ordered all the remaining warships at La Spezia scuttled paying special attention to the submarines of Decima MAS, the special forces unit responsible for sinking a score of Allied vessels, including two battleships. The pro-German sentiments of their leader, Commander Prince Junio Valerio Borghese, were well known and the admiral feared he might create an incident that could jeopardize the whole armistice. The Germans intervened trying to stop the destruction and the German admiralty in Berlin ordered Maranghini shot, but the German general at the scene ignored this directive considering the Italian admiral's actions legitimate.[51]

---

[49] Badoglio, *Italy in the Second World War*, 82.
[50] Renzo De Felice, *Mussolini l'alleato* (Turin: Einaudi, 1997), 35-37.
[51] Gerhard Schreiber, *I militari italiani nei campi di concentramento del Terzo Reich 1943-1945* (Rome: Ufficio Storico Stato Maggiore dell'Esercito, 1992), 145-46.

In the hours after the armistice there had been many encounters between Italian and German forces, but the first meeting between Italian and Allied naval units did not occur until a few minutes past 0800 on 9 September when the Italian submarine *Nichelio* surfaced off Salerno in accordance with orders she had received the night before. Within minutes three Royal Navy motor launches accosted her.

Figure 16. The submarine *Nichelio* surfaced off Salerno morning 9 September surrounded by British vessels vainly demanding her surrender. (Aria alla rapida)

One of the British boats motored alongside and her commander shouted "You are prisoners." He then threw a bundled Union Jack up on the submarine's sail and tried to explain with gestures that he expected the Italians to raise this flag above their own. The Italian captain ignored the pantomime, re-bundled the package and threw it back. Twice the flag went from motor launch to submarine and back again. Tensions grew and machine guns were manned on both sides. At the third toss the flag fell in the water, opened and sank as both sides silently watched. Then the Italian captain said he wanted to speak to the admiral in command. The British decided this was a good idea and escorted the submarine alongside Admiral Kent Hewitt's flagship, USS *Ancon*. The Italian captain told his XO to scuttle the boat if he did not return after two hours and, strapping on a pistol to emphasize that he was no one's prisoner, he boarded *Ancon*. The lieutenant's fears proved baseless as Admiral Hewitt welcomed the Italian submariner and accepted his word that he would not undertake any unprovoked hostile acts. No Allied sailor boarded *Nichelio*, while the Italians were allowed to visit *Ancon*, including the submarine's dog, which received cheers from the American sailors and, along with *Nichelio*'s crew, demonstrated an appreciation for American chow.[52]

The navy's immediate response to the armistice had resulted in the escape of most major units from German control; individual units, even in the absence of orders, had reacted forcefully and in some cases had defeated German aggression. However, it was a different situation with the army. Due to the leadership vacuum in Rome, 9 September developed as the most tragic day in the Italian army's history. Before dawn Italy's scattered commands from France to Greece, receiving news of the armistice, began phoning the ministry seeking instructions. Unfortunately, a clear policy was not forthcoming. Ultimately, General Ambrosio, who anticipated that all clashes would be local and that it would be best to minimize conflict before the German army began its inevitable withdrawal, was responsible for this command failure.[53]

With no direction from the top, conflicting orders emanated from various commands. As one soldier remembered, "There was a flood of orders, but each one was different ... resist the Germans; don't fire on the Germans; don't let the Germans disarm you; kill the Germans; lay down your weapons; don't give up your weapons."[54] On the peninsula, cases of army resistance to the Germans were scattered, with nothing greater than battalion-sized units holding out for a day or two. In Greece the local commands on Crete, Rhodes, and the mainland came to terms with the Germans after some scattered fighting, which resulted in the surrender of the warships at Piraeus and Suda Bay, as already related. The 11th Army command in Greece endorsed these accommodations and extended them the next day to the Albanian base of Durazzo, which was under the threat of German anti-aircraft batteries on the hills surrounding the harbor.

---

[52] Tullio Marcon, "Union Jack a mare!" *Aria alla rapida* (March 2004): 14-15.
[53] Zangrandi, *L'Italia tradita*, 441-59.
[54] Agarossi, *A Nation Collapses*, 105.

Figure 17. The captain of *Nichelio*, still wearing his pistol, leaving USS *Ancon* preceeded by the Royal Navy Volunteer Reserve lieutenant, presumably skipper of one of the motor launches that demanded *Nichelio*'s surrender. (U.S. Navy 80-G-87397)

In the Dodecanese Rhodes was the center of both Italian and German strength, and there hung the fate of the entire archipelago. On 9 September two British agents parachuted onto the island to encourage the governor, Admiral Inigo Campioni, and his thirty-thousand-man garrison to fight the seventy-five hundred Germans stationed there. Although shooting had already started, Campioni balked at the enticements of his ex-enemies and, as an Italian naval officer complained to one of the agents, the Italian troops "were not good and were shockingly led."[55] Campioni finally surrendered to the Germans on 11 September. They delivered him to Mussolini, who had the admiral shot for treason in May 1944. On the other islands the Italians generally cooperated with British troops, but not always with enthusiasm, although Italian manned batteries inflicted heavy casualties and even repulsed one German landing attempt against Leros. In the end the Germans reconquered the entire Dodecanese, executing many Italian officers and sending most of the captives to camps in Germany.[56]

The final Balkan balance sheet saw 300,000 Italians become German prisoners; about 9,000 died fighting the Wehrmacht; more than 6,000 were shot after capture; 13,300 died as POWs in transit from the Greek islands on German vessels sunk by Allied warships. Overall, more than 160,000 troops (half of them "black shirts") joined the Germans or Mussolini's new RSI state; this equated to about 15 percent of the enlisted personnel and 30 percent of the officers. About the same percent among the POWs in Allied hands refused to collaborate as workers after the 8 September 1943 armistice and remained prisoners.[57]

---

[55] Anthony Rogers, *Churchill's Folly: Leros and the Aegean* (London: Cassell, 2003), 35.

[56] For accounts of the Aegean campaign see Rogers, *Churchill's Folly*; Vincent P. O'Hara, *Struggle for the Middle Sea* (Annapolis, Naval Institute Press, 2009), 229-39; and Peter Schenk. *Kampf un die Ägäis* (Hamburg: E. S. Mittler & Sohn, 2000).

[57] Gabrio Lombardi, *L'8 settembre fuori d'Italia* (Milan: Mursia, 1967). For more information regarding the conflicts between the Italian and German armies see, Emilio Faldella, "La resistenza degli italiani all'Elba," *Storia Illustrata* (September 1973); Emilio Faldella, *L'Italia e la seconda guerra mondiale* (Bologna: Cappelli, 1960); Piero Fortuna, "Quella notte al Brennero," *Storia Illustrata* (September 1983); Marco Mattioli, "Operazione Centro Marte," *Storia e Battaglie* (June 2008); Rex Trye, *Mussolini's Soldiers* (Osceola, Wisc.: Motorbooks International, 1995), 154-55; *Saggi di Storia Etico-Militare* (Rome: Ufficio Storico Stato Maggiore Esercito, 1976) and *Memorie Storico Militari* (Rome: 1977).

Given the confusion and the collapse of army discipline from the top down, the negotiation of separate truces with the Germans in Italy and the Balkans was hardly remarkable, especially since significant elements regarded the Germans as comrades in arms and the armistice as dishonorable. By 12 September the general surrender of Italian formations in the German controlled portions of the Kingdom was accomplished, almost always, as in Rome, with formal honors, which did not prevent the Germans from arresting whosoever they chose after the ceremony.[58]

Figure 18. Some of the more than 20,000 Italian troops interned in Switzerland on September 1943 two days after the armistice declaration. (Storia Illustrata)

---

[58] See Filippini Massimo, *I caduti di Cefalonia: fine di un mito* (Rome: IBN, 2008).

CHAPTER 6. NO SAFE HAVENS

As the army disintegrated, Admiral Luigi Sansonetti, the navy's deputy chief of staff, remained in Rome struggling to run Supermarina amid the growing chaos. De Courten had left orders for the navy to cease hostilities and concentrate in bases under Italian control, despite instructions issued by Admiral Andrew Cunningham, Allied naval commander in chief in the Mediterranean, and delivered to Comando Supremo five days before that the Italian fleet should make for North Africa. Thus, De Courten had ordered the battle fleet to sail for La Maddalena, the battleships *Doria* and *Duilio* to remain at Taranto and the training battleship *Cesare* to transfer from Pola to Cattaro in Dalmatia. On the afternoon of 10 September, when hopes of maintaining control of Dalmatia proved unfounded, *Cesare* sailed for Taranto. On *Cesare* and *Doria* there were demonstrations against the armistice, but the captains settled these affairs peacefully.[59]

The fleet commander at Taranto, Admiral Alberto da Zara, and most of his officers wanted to scuttle their ships, and early on the 9th the battleships began sending all but skeleton crews ashore. Then around 1000 rumors arrived that German paratroopers were marching unopposed towards Taranto. This information (even if false, as they were advancing toward Bari) caused Sansonetti to order the ships to Malta to prevent them from falling into German hands. Da Zara hesitated to take this drastic step, but finally the arguments of the base commander, Admiral Giuseppe Fioravanzo, convinced him that the ships were more useful afloat than on the bottom—as long as Italy retained control. Moreover, Fioravanzo argued that scuttling would only grant Britain the decisive victory it had failed to win during the war.

Da Zara finally sailed at 1618, leaving behind two destroyers and some torpedo boats for local defense. Exiting the swept channel he sighted an Allied squadron approaching. This force, commanded by Vice Admiral Arthur Power, consisted of the battleships *King George V* and *Howe*, five cruisers, the fast mi-

---

[59] Ferruccio Botti, "L'8 Settembre 1943 sulla corazzata *Giulio Cesare*," *Storia Militare*, (December 1993).

nelayer *Abdiel* and a destroyer flotilla carrying elements of the British 1st Paratroop Division and a commando unit. Supermarina had only learned some two hours earlier that the British intended to land troops at Taranto. When Admiral Power entered the harbor he discovered the destroyers *FR23* and *Granatiere* and the torpedo boats *Sirio, Clio* and *Aretusa* with their torpedo tubes casually trained towards his battleships. Tension grew that night when an underwater explosion sank *Abdiel*. At first it was supposed that the ship had been victim of a delayed-action bomb dropped some nights before by RAF bombers. Days later the Italians discovered that the German MTBs *S54* and *S61* had laid some mines as they surreptitiously slipped out of the harbor during the chaotic night following the armistice.

Sansonetti's decision to order da Zara to sail for Malta was not an easy one, but it was made following the German occupation of La Spezia, Trieste, Genoa, Civitavecchia and Gaeta that same morning and before he learned of Admiral Power's mission. Da Courten had ordered only "a loyal execution of the armistice" and he disavowed Sansonetti's actions when he encountered his second-in-command again on 18 October 1943, after Sansonetti escaped the Germans by making a twenty-three day trek to the south.[60] However, the fact that at 1856 four Luftwaffe FW 190 fighter-bombers vainly attacked *Duilio* helped convince da Zara, at least, that Sansonetti's orders were correct.[61]

Worse news was, in any case, flooding into Supermarina's situation room. At noon Brandenburger commandos mounted a surprise attack against the La Maddalena naval base, capturing its commander, Admiral Bruto Brivonesi and compelling him to sign a truce with the commander of the German 90th Division an hour later. Concern grew as unreliable black shirts of the MILMART (*Milizia Artiglieria Marittima*) manned some of the naval base's batteries.

As La Maddalena fell German and Italian forces clashed on both extremes of the Adriatic Sea. At Venice, the torpedo boat *Audace* stopped the German motor torpedo-boats *S30* and *S33* from interfering with liners evacuating the personnel and the cadets of the naval academy to Brindisi. Meanwhile, at Cape

---

[60] De Courten, *Le Memorie*, 384.
[61] Alberto da Zara, *Pelle d'ammiraglio* (Verona: Mondadori, 1949), 421-22.

Santa Maria di Leuca in southern Puglie, *S54* and *S61,* with the landing craft *F478,* sank the Italian auxiliary minesweeper *Vulcania*. Further east, off Rhodes, Italian naval units seized the small German steamship *Taganrog*. The ship departed for Samos under Italian colors early the next morning.

Figure 19. Morning of 9 September, the auxiliary minesweeper *Vulcania* under the guns of S54 and S61 just before being scuttled (Erminio Bagnasco)

At 1316 Sansonetti made another difficult decision. With La Maddalena in unfriendly hands, there was no harbor in the Tyrrhenian Sea capable of receiving the battleships; thus, he reluctantly ordered the fleet to sail for Bone while he diverted the *Squadretta* from La Maddalena to Portoferraio in Elba. Supermarina also ordered the submarines (which had already received general instruction to stop hostilities and to sail north giving their position) to likewise sail for Allied controlled harbors. Contrary to Allied instructions, he had already ordered any freighters at sea to proceed to their scheduled destinations.[62]

On his initiative Sansonetti added to the Allied instructions, being broadcast since 1300, the following sentence, "Remember that the surrender of the ships or the hauling down of the ensign is not specified in the armistice terms."

---

[62] Giuseppe Fioravanzo, *La Marina dall'8 settembre 1943 alla fine del conflitto*.

Sansonetti admitted after the war this was a free interpretation. He went further at 1349 ordering units "to sink all German vessels ferrying troops from Sardinia to Corsica." This completely contradicted General Ambrosio's orders issued the night of 8/9 September to permit German landing craft to ferry troops from Sardinia to Corsica. Sansonetti repeated three times over the next four hours his orders for the battle fleet to sail for Bone, but Admiral Bergamini aboard *Roma* never answered.[63]

As the battle fleet navigated down Corsica's west coast, actions between Italian and German naval units increased in frequency. At 1427 off Terracina south of Rome the corvettes *Folaga, Ape* and *Cormorano* attacked five German barges, sinking *F345* and forcing the others ashore. While this skirmish was underway, the light cruiser *Scipione*, in a sortie from Taranto to escort the corvette *Baionetta* from Ortona, approached *S54, S61* and *F478*. The MTBs quickly evacuated the barge, and fled, leaving *F478* to sink. At the same time the waters around Leghorn saw a flurry of activity. Two German motor minesweepers attacked the submarine chasers *VAS234* and *235* off the Gorgona Islands. In an intense, hour-long action Rear Admiral Federico Martinengo, commander of the coastal anti-submarine warfare forces, died at the wheel of *VAS234* after the helmsman was killed, hit by the last enemy salvos just before the Germans fled. A fire destroyed the subchaser an hour later. Meanwhile, off Leghorn five German MTBs captured the Italian subchasers *VAS238, 239* and *305* and the landing craft *MZ709* and *740*; *MZ703* scuttled herself at the end of the action. At 1440 off Castiglioncello south of Leghorn the German minelayers *Brandenburg* and *Pommern*, supported by self-propelled artillery ashore, attacked the Italian auxiliary cruiser *Piero Foscari* and the steamer *Valverde*. The two Italian ships were stranded and lost. Moving north *Brandenburg* and *Pommern*, still enjoying artillery support, captured the Italian minelayer *Buffoluto* off Leghorn following a long gun duel.

These actions paled into insignificance, however, compared to the tragedy that struck the Regia Marina next. At 1530 twenty-eight Do.217 Luftwaffe bombers armed with the recently introduced FX-1400 airborne guided-bomb at-

---

[63] Gino Galuppini, "Pennello nero, part one," *Storia Militare* (August 1997).

tacked the Italian battle fleet in the Bocche di Bonifacio. One bomb penetrated the hull of Bergamini's flagship *Roma* and the resulting explosion knocked the aft engines off line. Another struck *Roma* a few minutes later and left the ship dead in the water and with a serious fire burning forward. This fire raged out of control and detonated the forward magazine. A massive explosion followed. The new battleship broke in two and sank at 1611, taking with her Admiral Bergamini and 1,252 of his men. A bomb also exploded off the bow of *Italia* (the former *Littorio*) wounding one man and causing some minor flooding. The navy had asked the Regia Aeronautica for an escort, but the Macchi C.202 fighters dispatched failed to find the fleet. During the German attack the Italian battleships catapulted one of their two Re.2000 fighters, but the plane could not climb to height in time to do any good and later landed in Corsica.

Figure 20. *Roma* afternoon of 9 September. This first photo shows the effect of the explosion that sent a column of dense smoke thousands of feet into the air. (Erminio Bagnasco)

Figure 21. This photo was taken at 1610 showing the 1,600 ton number 2 turret being blown overboard by the power of the magazine explosion. (Imperial War Museum)

Figure 22. This photo, taken four minutes after the preceding one, shows the ship, her keel broken, sinking. (Imperial War Museum)

Roma's destruction did not clarify the situation for the Italians. A report broadcast to Supermarina at 1617 stated, "Battle force attacked by English planes stop battleship *Roma* hit and in danger of sinking."[64] Considering that before noon the cruiser *Eugenio di Savoia* had fired upon a British reconnaissance plane

---

[64] Gino Galuppini, "Pennello nero, part two," *Storia Militare* (September 1997).

that was shadowing the battle fleet, the mistake was natural, and indicated that Bergamini still regarded the Allies as hostile.

For their part, the Allies were confused about the Italian fleet's intentions. Signal intelligence decoded an intercepted message at 1514 on the 9th indicating the fleet's destination was La Maddalena, while in his memoirs Admiral Cunningham wrote: "For some reason that was never quite clear to me, though some said the orders were issued by the Germans in the name of the Italian Admiralty, the fleet turned east into the Gulf of Asinara, in the north of Sardinia, instead of making their way south with all dispatch."[65]

At 1649 Admiral Luigi Biancheri, commander of the VIII Division (cruisers *Garibaldi* and *Abruzzi*) suggested to the new senior officer, Admiral Romeo Oliva, commander of the VII Division (cruisers *Eugenio di Savoia*, *Aosta* and *Montecuccoli*) that the fleet return to La Spezia. Oliva, however, preferred to head west trying to discover what had really happened while the cruiser *Regolo*, the destroyers *Mitragliere*, *Fuciliere* and *Carabiniere* and the torpedo boats *Orsa*, *Pegaso* and *Impetuoso* rescued the battleship's survivors. They proceeded to Minorca in the Balearic Islands where they landed the wounded on 10 September. Here *Pegaso* and *Impetuoso* scuttled on 11 September while the others remained in limbo, not interned but almost without fuel, until 15 January 1945, when they were finally returned to Italy.

As the battle fleet regrouped, the destroyers *Vivaldi* and *Da Noli* approached the narrows between Sardinia and Corsica from the east. At 1650 they attacked a German motor minesweeper and three landing craft in the narrows, forcing the barges ashore. Bonifacio's shore batteries, which the black shirts had handed over to the Germans that morning, engaged and damaged both destroyers. Then *Da Noli* hit a mine and sank; a German bomber damaged *Vivaldi* and she foundered the next day.

---

[65] Andrew Browne Cunningham, *A Sailor's Odyssey* (London: Hutchinson, 1951), 563 and TNA, ADM223, file 585, ZIP/ZTPI/37708. This signal was sent immediately to Cunningham's headquarters at Algiers.

At 2124 Admiral Oliva clarified to Rome that German, not British, planes had attacked the fleet. A very long night followed before, on 10 September at 0449, the new flagship ordered a course set for Bone.

Figure 23. Admiral Romeo Oliva. He took command of the battle fleet after the sinking of *Roma* and ultimately made the decision to take the fleet to Malta. (Rivista Marittima)

Chapter 7. A Gentlemen's Agreement.

Da Zara with *Duilio* and *Doria*, the cruiser *Cadorna* and the destroyer *Da Recco* arrived off Malta on 10 September at around 0930. At 1700 the Italian ships filed into Grand Harbor where British boarding parties, each consisting of an Italian-speaking officer and a dozen sailors, awaited them. They instructed the Italians to remove the torpedo pistols and the breeches on all the guns, except A/A weapons; to disable the floatplanes; to concentrate all hand weapons on the stern; and to seal the radio rooms. These things da Zara's men refused to do. Supermarina's instructions issued the day before authorized the presence of a British boarding party "to oversee compliance with the armistice terms," but did not grant the British access below decks. The weapons remained under Italian supervision (only *Da Recco*, laying in an isolated bay separated from the rest of the squadron, surrendered the blocks of her crew's rifles, but they were restored the next day).[66]

The British finally accepted the word of the ships' captains they would not act against the Allies; the same solution was adopted for the guns, the torpedoes and the scuttling charges. Tensions flared when a British party tried to remove a battleship's radio antennas, but at last an uneasy balance was established and the night and the day after passed without trouble, helped by the polite attitude of the boarding party commanders who had orders to avoid incidents.

On 10 September at 0838 as da Zara's squadron neared Malta, Admiral Oliva's fleet sighted a British squadron (the battleships *Warspite* and *Valiant* and seven destroyers). Captain T.M. Brownrigg of Cunningham's staff boarded the new flagship *Eugenio* at 0910, after asking permission, and offered assistance for *Italia*'s damage. This gesture, reinforced by the proper behavior of the Allied crews (in contrast to the jeers that greeted the German fleet on 21 November 1918 when it was forced to stream between lines of British warships on its way to interment at Scapa Flow) had a calming effect. Eisenhower's naval aide noted that, "As Brownrigg and Smith were seen to board the *Savoia* [sic] and all ap-

---

[66] Giuseppe del Minio, "Memorie di un comandante di cacciatorpediniere" *Il mare*, (June 1959).

peared serene, the tension was relaxed, and from gun turrets came smiles and cameras."[67]

Figure 24. Da Zara reviewing an honor guard from HMS *Warspite* before getting in the car for his round-about tour of Malta. (Erminio Bagnasco)

At 1500, off Bizerte, Admiral Cunningham, who was flying his flag on the destroyer HMS *Hambledon* with General Eisenhower aboard as an observer (rather than overseeing the touch-and-go situation at Salerno from a location with better communications, a demonstration of the importance the Allies attached to this event) signaled the Italian flagship his regrets for the loss of *Roma*. These courtesies made the difficult task of entering Malta on the morning of 11 September more palatable, although Oliva had to reject another proposal by Admiral Biancheri to scuttle the ships once they were moored in Grand Harbor. The British did not require Oliva's ships to accept boarding parties.

---

[67] Harry C. Butcher, *My Three Years with Eisenhower: The Personal Diary of Captain Harry C. Butcher, USNR Naval Aide to General Eisenhower, 1942 to 1945* (New York: Simon and Schuster, 1946), 414.

The following afternoon Cunningham met with Admiral da Zara, the senior Regia Marina officer at Malta. The British commander greeted his counterpart with full military honors. At the conference Cunningham accepted da Zara's word that his men would respect the Armistice and declared that the boarding parties would be withdrawn at sunset. Finally Cunningham accompanied his former enemy back to his car and saluted him adding at the last second, as he placed a hand on his shoulder, "Yours is a very difficult job, Admiral."[68] However, despite his outward courtesy, the politically astute Cunningham could not resist some theatrics: "My office was no more than about sixty steps up a circular stairway; but I though it advisable that da Zara should see something of what the Axis airmen had done to Malta, and also that the Maltese should see him. Accordingly we had him brought a roundabout way by car."[69]

After this meeting Cunningham sent his oft-quoted signal to the Admiralty, "Be pleased to inform their Lordships that the Italian Battle fleet now lays at anchor under the guns of the fortress of Malta." These famous words disguised the fact that the British did not have physical control over the former enemy fleet. The Americans especially appreciated the irony. When Admiral di Pollone's *Squadretta* unexpectedly arrived at Palermo from the island of Elba, at 1000 on 12 September, the American commander there felt like signaling, "Be pleased to inform Their Lordships that Palermo lies under the guns of an Italian Fleet."[72] The British lack of control was further indicated by a letter Cunningham sent to Admiral Willis on 14 September in which he worried, "[the Italian Fleet] is alright at the moment but I smell trouble coming. I am quite convinced that all the ships are prepared to scuttle should things not be to their liking."[73]

---

[68] Da Zara, *Pelle d'ammiraglio*, 426.
[69] Cunningham. *Sailors Odyssey*, 564.
[72] Quoted in Morison, *Sicily-Salerno-Anzio*, 244.
[73] Michael Simpson, ed., *The Cunningham Papers*. Vol. 2, *The Triumph of Allied Sea Power 1942–1946* (Aldershot, England: Ashgate, 2006), 129.

Figure 25. Morning 11 September, the mustered crew of the battleship HMS *Warspite* watching *Italia* (Imperial War Museum)

Figure 26. Admirals Cunningham and Da Zara. (Erminio Bagnasco)

Figure 27. On 11 September the light cruiser *Eugenio di Savoia*, flagship of Admiral Romeo Oliva arrives at Malta. (Erminio Bagnasco)

Figure 28. *Vittorio Veneto* at Malta. (Erminio Bagnasco)

The important facts about the passage of the Italian battleships to Malta were, therefore, first, that it was not a surrender, but an operation ordered by the Italian high command in response to German attacks or threats; second that once the fleet was at Malta, the British exercised no control over it; and third, that da Zara did not know the text of the Armistice, nor did he enjoy Supermarina's support (which made its last broadcast at 1709 on 10 September following the truce between the Germans and Caviglia's emissaries). Even if da Zara personally favored a partnership with the Anglo-Americans he had to make decisions affecting the navy's most powerful units for two difficult weeks without instructions.

Figure 29. Da Zara introducing his officers to Commander Dick of Admiral Cunningham's staff at the Custom House Steps in Malta, 11 September. (Erminio Bagnasco)

As Italian admirals decided matters of policy, King Victor Emmanuel, Badoglio and Ambrosio, with De Courten, Sandalli and a bevy of generals, crowded aboard the corvette *Baionetta* in the small Adriatic harbor of Ortona at 0110 on 10 September for a fifteen hour voyage to Brindisi. Upon arrival the exiles found conditions difficult. There were no facilities or proper lodgings for such an illustrious influx and Radio Brindisi was too weak to permit communications with the entire nation.

At sea the fighting between Italian and German forces continued. On 10 September at 0630 off Civitavecchia the MFPs *F513*, *F514*, *F542* and *F554* clashed briefly with *VAS247* and *248*. At La Maddalena an Italian battery sank a small landing boat that approached too near the gun emplacements. This did not spark a general confrontation because the commander of the German 90th Division admitted his men had violated the shaky local truce. In the Adriatic five German aircraft ineffectively bombed *Cesare* as she sailed for Taranto. In the Western Mediterranean, off Capo Carbonara, an USAAF bomber sank the Italian submarine *Topazio* with all hands. The aircraft crew said she was not displaying a black pennant.

A major battle took place at Piombino which remained critically important to the Germans due to their planned evacuation of Corsica and Sardinia.

At 0200 on 10 September the torpedo boats *TA9* and *TA11* and the armed steamer *Carbet* appeared off the Tuscan port requesting permission to refuel.

After negotiations, the local army commander agreed as long as the Germans departed immediately after taking on supplies. At 0800 the torpedo boats moored so that their 100-mm guns covered the entire harbor.

Figure 30. The German torpedo boat *TA11*. Italian naval shore batteries at Piombino sank her on 10 September. (Erminio Bagnasco)

At 1140 *TA11* turned her weapons on *VAS208*, *214*, *219* and *220* entering the port and forced them to moor alongside, imprisoning their crews. At noon, the Germans had finished refueling, but they refused to leave. Hampered by desertions, the army was ready to cede the port, but the navy stated it required orders from Supermarina before it could surrender.

Throughout the day, German intentions became clear. At 1525 *F513*, *F514*, *F542* and *F554* arrived bringing troops from Civitaveccia. Two hours later *F420*, the motor minesweeper *R185* and seven barges with more soldier crowded into the harbor. It could have been worse as *Folaga* and *Ape* intercepted five MPFs off Elba at 1330 that day denying them access to the port. Still, by dark the Germans had concentrated at Piombino the two torpedo boats, an armed steamer, an R-boat, five MFPs, eight landing craft, two Luftwaffe air-rescue boats and four air force launches.

After dark, German patrols began infiltrating beyond the harbor. Trying to observe these movements, an Italian unit fired a rocket flare at 2045; this provoked gunfire. The torpedo boats began bombarding Italian positions and the shore batteries retaliated. The action proved too hot for *TA9* which, accompanied by *F554*, cast off after suffering several damaging hits from a 3-inch battery. She stood offshore and fired from outside the range of the smaller Italian guns. *TA11* engaged from her mooring at the south mole. An Italian shell struck one of the VAS boats tied alongside and ignited a fire. Oil floating on the water turned this into a conflagration that quickly enveloped the torpedo boat, which became a total loss. By 2200 *Carbet*, the air force boats, the captured VAS boats and two of the barges, *Mainz* and *Meise*, were all sunk.[76]

The Italians secured the port and the surviving German vessels were permitted to leave the next day. However, it was a short-lived victory as units of the 24th Panzer and 305th Infantry Divisions arrived on 12 September.

---

[76] See Alessandro Dondoli, "Piombino, settembre 1943," *Storia Militare* 72 (September 1999): 4-14.

CHAPTER 8. DEFEAT THROUGH DECEPTION?

Although in the first three days the Regia Marina's acceptance of the armistice had gone better than anyone could expect, British disregard for Italian sentiments began to fuel the lingering suspicion of many officers and men that the Allies had employed deception to obtain a cheap victory.

Suspicions first flared up on 10 September when the battleships *King George V* and *Howe* suddenly weighted anchor and departed Taranto. The Italians had construed their unexpected arrival and presence under the guns of Taranto's 12-in and 8-in batteries as a sort of guarantee of Allied goodwill and mutual respect of the Regia Marina's fleet. Their departure, along with looting and other undisciplined behavior by the commandos that landed at Taranto, led Admiral Sansonetti to suspect the British did not intend to respect the terms or spirit of the armistice. Next, the BBC aired a bombastic broadcast that declared that the Italian ships at Malta had ignominiously surrendered. Admiral Cunningham was quoted in the New York Times as saying that "the armistice provides we can do with [the Italian ships] as we like." The article also opined, "One gathered that Admiral Cunningham might have admired the Italians more if their navy had fought it out rather than surrendering."[77]

Such pronouncements threatened the working accommodation da Zara had just reached with Cunningham. They induced Grand Admiral di Revel and the former chiefs of staff, Admirals Domenico Cavagnari and Arturo Riccardi, with Admiral Angelo Iachino, the ex-fleet commander—all of whom had remained in Rome—to conclude that the Italian navy had been cheated and that it was honor bound to continue the fight on the German side, on a volunteer basis, due to the separation of the king, who very probably had been deceived too and was unable to express his will since he had left the royal palace and entered the walls of the army ministry.[78]

Not withstanding these conclusions by some of the navy's old leadership, clashes against the Germans continued. At 0400 on 11 September off Ancona in

---

[77] Clark Lee, "Our Leaders Hail Italian Fleet Gain." *New York Times* (12 September 1943).
[78] Romano Canosa, *Storia dell'epurazione in Italia* (Milan: Baldini e Castoldi, 1999), 77-90.

the Adriatic Sea the German motor torpedo-boats *S54* and *S61* torpedoed and sank the Italian gunboat *Aurora* and seized, at dawn, the motorship *Leopardi* crowded with hundreds of civilian passengers. *S54* and *S61* captured the steamer *Pontinia* later that day. They also ambushed and sank the destroyer *Sella*. At Castellamare di Stabia Germans troops attacked again and seized the town after *Giulio Germanico* ran out of ammunition. Finally, off Punta Olipa in the Adriatic German aircraft attacked and sank the small, pre-World War I torpedo boat *T8* in transit from Dubrovnik. At 1800 that evening her sister *T6* scuttled short of Rimini because she lacked fuel to reach a friendly port.

Figure 31. 11 September 1943. The battleship *Italia* flying a signal indicating a local pilot on board, about to drop anchor off Malta's Grand Harbor. (Erminio Bagnasco)

The revolt of the Regia Marina's beached admirals cracked the navy's hitherto united front. It split wide open three days later, on 14 September, when Decima MAS's Commander Borghese decided, after two days of negotiations, to fight on the Reich's side under the Italian flag, bringing his unit's personnel with him. The next day a collaboration agreement with the Kriegsmarine, supported by Grandadmiral Thaon di Revel, whose presidency of the Senate gave his action an institutional endorsement, laid the basis of what would soon become the navy of the new *Repubblica Sociale Italiana*, which grew from Prince Borghese's unit into an efficient 10,000-man coastal force that fought the Allies until 2 May 1945.

Events at Malta seemed to confirm the actions of those elements that elected to continue fighting alongside the Germans. On 15 September the British again demanded that da Zara's ships deactivate their guns, torpedoes and scuttling charges. The Italians again refused, disembarking only the now useless floatplanes and the last Re.2000 fighter and destroying all secret documents. The British suspended supplies and the Italians responded by rationing food and water. The fleet's endurance, estimated at twenty days, was enhanced, however, by the arrival of di Pollone's *Squadretta* on 20 September. The U.S. Navy had supplied the Italian ships during their Palermo stopover with huge quantities of luxury items like spam, dried eggs, flour, coffee and milk.[79]

One incident is reflective of the tensions. A few days after the meeting between Admirals da Zara and Cunningham, a boat ferried a Royal Navy captain to the cruiser *Garibaldi*. Her skipper, Giorgio Ghé, who was fluent in English, met the British officer and shared a vermouth with him in the wardroom. Afterwards, Captain Ghé called a meeting of his officers and advised that the British confirmed they could keep their anti aircraft guns and had even just provided them with the signals and the radio frequencies of Malta's air defense command. However, the main guns had to be disabled. One officer remembered:

"Our faces were quite dark. Captain Ghé then added that the British would collect the firing pins and the mood changed in a flash. The gunnery officer called the oldest of the gunnery NCOs, a Neapolitan giant who had been on board since before the ship's commissioning, and gave him the order in front of us to remove the pins. Not a single word was added, but I was able to see the light in the eyes of the couple. The giant made his trip inside the four 6-inch turrets with a little wooden box; then he passed the box to the officer who deli-

---

[79] Luciano Barca, *Buscando per mare con la Decima Mas* (Rimini: Riuniti, 2001), 93.

vered it to the captain who gave it to the British officer." His mission accomplished, the British officer exited. Then, "the NCO, with a thunderous voice which could be heard from bow to stern, addressed the gunnery officer, 'Asking permission to replace the pins,' adding in softer tone 'I always keep three full sets in case one of them breaks.'" Permission was granted and the incident was over.[80]

Figure 32. American troops visiting the corvette *Danaide* at Palermo on December 1943. (Storia Militare)

The British made similar demands on the main Italian battle force (battleships *Vittorio Veneto* and *Italia*, with four cruisers and four destroyers) when it arrived at Alexandria, escorted by *Howe* and *King George V* with a flotilla of destroyers, on the morning of 16 September. Here the Italians agreed to put the

---

[80] Federico Oriana, "Giuseppe Oriana", *Supplement of the Rivista Marittima* (June 2008): 29-30.

breeches of their main guns in the Italian consulate, which was under Swiss protection, as the French had done in the same harbor from July 1940 until May 1943. They refused, however, to give up the 6-inch guns (necessary to repulse any effort to board the ships) and the anti-aircraft weapons.

While these events occurred in Malta and Egypt, sporadic combat between German and Italian navy forces continued.

On 13 September, on the Ionian island of Cephalonia, a battery of the Acqui Division attacked a pair of German landing barges sinking *F495* and capturing the other. It also damaged three motor fishery vessels (MFVs). A bitter fight then developed which lasted until 21 September. The final act was the German murder of 355 Italian prisoners of war, mostly officers.[81] Hundreds of Italian officers who fell into German hands were likewise executed in Yugoslavia, Albania and after the capture of Corfu, Leros and Cos.[82]

At La Maddalena on 13 September, repeated incidents between 0930 and 1530 marred the local truce. The Germans attacked and seized the Italian landing ship *Garigliano* and Regia Marina batteries stopped the transfer of the 90th Division from Sardinia to Corsica. Italian naval personnel led by the base commander, Captain Carlo Avegno, who died during the action, recovered facilities occupied four days before by the Germans and rescued Admiral Brivonesi. The admiral negotiated a new local truce which lasted until 15 September. At Montecristo Island the corvettes *Gabbiano* and *Pellicano* engaged German landing craft and forced them ashore. At the same time, some miles away, the Italian submarine *H2* (a World War One Holland boat) fought a surface action with the German MTB *S158*. The German boat, being without torpedoes, tried to sink the submarine with machine gun fire, but was repulsed. On Corfu an Italian army battery engaged an MFP landing craft and five MFVs sinking the landing craft and two MFVs and damaging the other three. Off Corfu on the morning of 14 September a German air attack badly damaged the torpedo boat *Giuseppe Sirtori*. She ran aground and was finally destroyed on 25 September when the island fell to the Germans.

---

[81] See Gerhard Schreiber, *I militari italiani internati*.
[82] Erminio Bagnasco, *Corsari in Adriatico 8-13 settembre 1943* (Milan, Mursia, 2006).

Tensions remained high at La Maddalena. On 15, 16 and 17 September navy shore batteries harassed ferries transporting the 90th Division from Sardinia to Corsica. On 16 September the Regia Aeronautica undertook its first action against the Germans sending five CANT Z 1007 of the 88° Gruppo against the ferries. They sank one landing craft at the cost of one plane shot down. The next day the Germans completed their evacuation.

During the campaign in Dalmatia, Montenegro, Albania and the Ionian Islands that lasted until 5 October, the Regia Marina ferried home more than 25,000 men (in particular the Emilia Infantry Division and the San Marco Armored Cavalry Group) and 500 German prisoners. During these operations German air attacks sank the old torpedo boats *Stocco* and *Cosenz* on 24 and 27 September respectively as well as some freighters, tankers and minor vessels. The Italian air force entered the action from 18 September sinking the German landing craft *F331*, the MTB *LS6* and five small auxiliaries. No Allied planes intervened in the Ionian campaign until 27 September. On 30 September the Germans seized Porto Palermo, the last Albanian harbor held by Italian forces. The campaign in the Aegean islands began on 8 September and lasted until 28 November. The Italian navy lost the destroyer *Euro* and some minor vessels there, fighting alongside the British in a losing cause.[83]

---

[83] For information regarding these actions see Giuseppe Fioravanzo, *La Marina italiana dall' 8 settembre 1943 alla fine del conflitto*; Giuseppe Fioravanzo, *La Marina nella Guerra di Liberazione e nella Resistenza* (Rome, Ufficio Storico della Marina Militare, 1995); Giorgio Franconi, "Una corvetta della Regia Marina attraverso l'armistizio," *Storia Militare* (July 1998); Zvonimir Freivogel, "Siluranti ex italiane sotto bandiera tedesca." *Storia Militare* 36 (September 1996): 18–29; and 37 (October 1996): 22–35; Manfred Krellenberg, "L' affondamento dell'Elbano Gasperi," *Storia Militare* (May 1999); A. Levi, *Avvenimenti in Egeo dopo l'armistizio* (Rome: Ufficio Storico della Marina Militare: 1972).

Figure 33. *Impavido* at Portoferraio in late September 1943 after the surrender of Elba to the Germans. (Storia Militare)

Figure 34. 5 October 1943 the corvette *Gabbiano* returning to Taranto from Malta. (Erminio Bagnasco)

CHAPTER 9. ON THE KNEES OF THE GODS.

An Allied mission visited the Italian government in Brindisi on 14 September. While Eisenhower had little cause to complain about the actions of the Italian navy, he was gravely disappointed that the army had not delivered the cooperation Castellano had promised—particularly at Rome, where it seemed six divisions had folded in the face of two German divisions and in the islands where, as Eisenhower wrote to General Marshall, "In both [Corsica and Sardinia] they had the strength to kick the Germans into the sea. Instead they have apparently done nothing."[84] Italy's leaders made a mixed impression. The king seemed, "pathetic," Badoglio was "old, benevolent, honest and very friendly ..." Ambrosio was "intelligent and friendly," but "depressed and lacking in enthusiasm."[85]

Figure 35. Marshal Badoglio, General Rossi and General Castellano 14 September at Brindisi sitting on a bench outside the submarine barrarks. (Mondadori)

---

[84] Garland and McGaw Smyth, *Sicily and the Surrender of Italy*, 541.
[85] Ibid., 542.

As a consequence of the Salerno crisis General Eisenhower quickly realized that the prospect of a swift and happy ending to the Italian campaign was, at best, remote, and after the Brindisi mission he decided to again propose his original program for Italian co-belligerency against the Germans. The idea was debated at Washington and approved by President Roosevelt on 17 September and accepted, somewhat grudgingly, by the British. The first positive movement toward establishing the legal framework for this status occurred three weeks before Italy's declaration of war against Germany. Not surprisingly, it came from the navy.

On 23 September Admirals Cunningham and De Courten signed an agreement at Taranto which ended the Italo-British war of nerves. The agreement specified that an armistice having been signed, and given the wish of the King of Italy and the Italian Government "to assist in the prosecution of the war with the Axis powers," that the battleships would be placed on a care and maintenance basis, that at least one squadron of cruisers would be kept in commission and the balance in care and maintenance, that all destroyers, torpedo boats and small coastal craft would be kept in commission and that submarines would be immobilized in port and brought into service as required. "Under this modification of the armistice terms, all Italian ships will continue to fly their flags. A large proportion of the Italian Navy will thus remain in active commission operating their own ships and fighting alongside the forces of the UN against the Axis powers."[86]

Establishing naval collaboration against the Germans allowed De Courten to at last contact da Zara and confirm some of his previous actions, such as dispatching the destroyers *Legionario* and *Oriani* to Algiers on 13 September to ferry an American OSS unit to Corsica to assist the Italian troops fighting the Germans there.

The failure of Italy's military and political leadership in terminating their alliance with Germany and arranging an armistice with the Allies can be meas-

---

[86] Quoted from the Memorandum of Agreement on the Employment and Disposition of the Italian Fleet and Mercantile Marine between the Allied Naval C-in-C, acting on behalf of the Allied C-in-C, and the Italian Minister of Marine. See Simpson, *Cunningham Papers Volume II*, 131-33.

ured by the consequences. The nation became a bloody battleground suffering the death of nearly 260,000 citizens—150,000 of them civilians—killed not only as a side effect of the world war, but in Italy's own violent civil war. Germany occupied and looted the north, while the Allies climbed slowly from the south to the Alps ravaging by battle and bomber much of the country in the process.

Although German commandos rescued Mussolini on 12 September and Hitler allowed him to establish the co-called *Repubblica Sociale Italiana*, he exercised little power and an Italian partisan killed him on 28 April 1945 a day after he had been captured while fleeing north. King Victor Emmanuel, in a vain attempt to save the House of Savoy, abdicated in May 1946 in favor of Crown Prince Umberto, one month before a referendum on whether Italy should remain a kingdom or become a republic. Fifty-four percent voted for the republic. Victor Emmanuel died a year later in exile in Alexandria, Egypt. Marshal Badoglio continued as prime minister presiding over Italy's declaration of war against German on 13 October 1943. Prince Umberto dismissed him in June 1944 following the liberation of Rome to permit the formation of a new government. He was never tried for any war crimes and died eleven years later at an advanced age.

In 1944 Italian legend held that Admiral Bergamini, proclaimed the following words on *Roma*'s bridge the evening before his death: "This is not what we imagined would be the end, but this is the course by which we must now steer. ... The day will come when this living force of the Navy will be the cornerstone on which the Italian people will be enabled to rebuild their fortunes." According to a witness he actually said: "It might be that our ships will be attacked by both the Anglo-Americans and the Germans ... but in any case they will not be seized by anyone."[87] Both speeches, however, express a certain truth. The navy's personnel—admirals, officers, NCOs and ratings—acted according to well-founded principles. The Regia Marina was the one institution of the Italian state that emerged from the national debacle of the armistice largely intact. Its reputation has been darkened by unsympathic histories but, in fact, the brand of

---

[87] Gino Galuppini, "Il discorso dell'ammiraglio Bergamini," *Bollettino d'archivio dell'Ufficio Storico della Marina Militare* (June 1998), 97-110.

"Dark Navy" is one of honor. It never surrendered and never failed to obey orders.

Figure 36. Malta 29 September 1943. Marshal Badoglio in front with Eisenhower following to the right aboard HMS *Nelson* to sign the "long terms." From the left, General John Gort, governor of Malta, Air Marshal Arthur Tedder, General Arthur Coningham and Marshal Harold Alexander at the extreme right. (Erminio Bagnasco)

Figure 37. September 12, 1943. Mussolini rescued by German troops. (Signal Magazine)

Figure 38. The price paid. Italian naval prisoners from the Aegean arriving at Versen Stammlager two days before Christmas, 1943. (Ferruccio Ferrucci)

Appendix I. Operational Italian naval vessels by location as of 8 Sep. 1943[88]

Tyrrhenian Sea

At Sea: Submarines: *Alagi, Diaspro, Galatea, Topazio, Turchese, Marea, Vortice, Brin, Giada, Nichelio, Platino*

La Spezia

Battleships: *Roma, Vittorio Veneto, Italia*

Cruisers: *Eugenio di Savoia, Regolo, Aosta*

Destroyers: *Grecale, Velite, Mitragliere, Carabiniere, Fuciliere, Legionario, Artigliere, Oriani, Vivaldi, Da Noli*

Torpedo Boats: *Ardimentoso, Pegaso, Orsa, Orione, Ariete, Impetuoso, Indomito, Mosto, Carini,*

Corvette: *Folaga*

Genoa

Cruisers: *Garibaldi, Abruzzi, Montecuccoli*

Torpedo Boats: *Libra, Animoso*

Bastia, Corsica

Torpedo Boats: *Aliseo, Ardito*

Corvette: *Cormorano*

Bonifacio, Corsica

Submarines: *H6, Rismondo*

Ajaccio, Corsica:

Submarines: *H1, H2, H4*

La Maddalena

---

[88] For order of battle details see Erminio Bagnasco, *In guerra Sul Mare: Navi e marinai italiani nel secondo conflitto mondiale* (Parma: Ermanno Albertelli, 2005), 388-92; Giuseppe Bernardi, *La Marina, gli armistizi e il trattato di pace* (Rome: Ufficio Storico della Marina Militare, 1979); Giuseppe Fioravanzo, *La Marina italiana dall' 8 settembre 1943 alla fine del conflitto* (Rome: Ufficio Storico della Marina Militare, 1971); Franco Bargoni, *Esploratori, fregate, avvisi e corvette* (Rome: Ufficio Storico della Marina Militare, 1974).

Corvettes: *Minerva, Danaide*

Submarine: *Corridoni*

Portoferraio

Corvette: *Ape*

Pozzuoli

Torpedo Boats: *Calliope, Fortunale, Fabrizi*

Corvette: *Vespa*

Gaeta

Corvettes: *Gabbiano, Pellicano, Gru*

Submarine: *Axum*

Porto Conte, Sardinia

Corvette: *Ibis*

Ionian Sea

At Sea: Submarines: *Bragadin, Menotti, Settembrini, Zoea, Onice, Bandiera, Jalea, Squalo*

Taranto

Battleships: *Duilio, Doria*

Cruisers: *Cadorna, Scipione, Pompeo*

Destroyers: *Da Recco, FR23, Granatiere*

Torpedo Boats: *Sirio, Clio, Aretusa*

Corvette: *Flora*

Submarine: *Atropo*

Adriatic Sea

At Sea: Destroyer: *Riboty* (in transit from Venice to Bari)

Pola

Battleship: *Cesare**

Torpedo Boats: *Sagittario, Insidioso*

Corvettes: *Baionetta,* Urania**

Venice

Destroyer: *Sella**

Torpedo Boat: *Audace*
Trieste
Corvette: *Berenice*
Brindisi
Torpedo Boats: *Sirtori, Stocco, Cosenz*
Corvettes: *Pomona, Chimera, Sibilla, Fenice*
Durazzo
Torpedo Boats: *Missori, Pilo*
Corvettes: *Sfinge, Scimitarra*
Cattaro
Torpedo Boat: *Abba*

Aegean Sea
At Sea: Torpedo Boat: *Monzambano* (in transit from Patrasso to Taranto)
Piraeus
Destroyers: *Crispi, Turbine*
Torpedo Boats: *San Martino, Calatafimi*
Suda
Torpedo Boats: *Solferino, Castelfidardo*
Leros
Destroyer: *Euro*

Beyond the Mediterranean Sea:
Bordeaux
Submarines: *Bagnolini,* *Finzi,* *CA2** (midget)
Danzig
Submarines: *S1,* *S2,* *S3,* *S4,* *S5,* *S6,* *S7,* *S8,* *S9**
Shanghai
Gunboats: *Lepanto, Carlotto*
Indian Ocean (at sea)
Submarine: *Cagni*

Colonial Sloop: *Eritrea*

Singapore

Submarines: *Giuliani,** *Torelli**

Sabang

Submarine: *Cappellini**

* = not fully operational

Appendix II. German naval vessels in the Mediterranean Sea on 9 Sep. 1943

Western Mediterranean

Torpedo Boats: *TA9, TA11*

MTB: *S56,* 58, 59, 60, 151, 152, 153, 154, 155, 156, 157, 158*

Subchasers: *UJ2203, 2206, 2207, 2208, 2209, 2210, 2211, 2214, 2215, 2216, 2218, 2219, 6070, 6071, 6075, 6078*

Motor minesweepers: *R1, 3, 4, 7, 8, 10,* 12, 13, 14, 15, 16, 39, 161, 162, 178, 185, 187, 188, 189, 190, 191, 192, 198, 199, 200, 201, 212, 215*

Submarines: *U73, 371, 380, 392, 410, 431, 453, 593, 616, 617, 731, 761, 960*

Transports: *KT2, 14, 16, 31*

Sloop: *SG11*

Minelayers: *Brandenburg, Pommern*

Fighter Direction Ship: *Kreta*

Minesweepers: 27

Support ships: 3

Eastern Mediterranean

Torpedo Boat: *TA10*

Subchasers: *UJ2101, 2102, 2104, 2105, 2107, 2108, 2109, 2110*

MTB: *S54, 61* (Taranto); *S30, 33* (Pola); *S36, 55* (Salamis); *LS5, 6* (Ionian Sea)

Motor minesweepers: *R34, 38, 40, 194, 195, 210, 211*

Submarines: *U81, 407, 565, 596*

Minelayers: *Drache, Bulgaria*

Transport: *KT6*

Minesweepers: 15

In the two theatres there were eighty-eight MFPs, about ten Siebel-Ferries and about fifty smaller infantry landingcraft of the *PiLb* and *Infantrielandungsboot* types, not including yard boats, and some Luftwaffe rescue motor launches.

Appendix III. Major Italian Warships Under Repair or Still Building on 8 Sep. 1943

(Includes only purpose built warships displacing more than 500 tons, armed with guns of 3.9-in or larger and capable of sixteen knots)

COMMISSIONED SHIPS UNDER REPAIR OR REFIT

Battleships

Cavour: Repairing at Trieste from torpedo damage inflicted at Taranto on 11 November 1940. Work halted on 22 June 1943 to give precedence to torpedo boats, MTBs and submarines. On 31 August 1943 *Cavour* was scheduled to be combat ready by late spring 1944. The Germans captured her and removed one triple turret in the winter of 1944/1945 intending to ship it to Bergen, Norway to serve as a shore battery. However, this was never done and the turret remained at Trieste. The RAF bombed *Cavour* on 17 February 1945 inflicting minor damage. A USAAF raid three days later sank her.

Cruisers

Gorizia: Repairing at La Spezia after being bombed by USAAF at La Maddalena on 10 April 1943 and scheduled to be operational by March 1944. The Germans salvaged what they could and the ship was then abandoned in the commercial harbor.

Bolzano: Repairing at La Spezia after being torpedoed on 13 August 1942 by the British submarine *Unbroken*. Priority had been given to *Gorizia* and she would not have been repaired before 1945. The Germans stripped her and she lay abandoned until sunk by a British chariot attack craft on 22 June 1944.

Taranto: Decommissioned at La Spezia on December 1942 to release personnel for the new escorts. The Italians scuttled her on 9 September. The German raised her, but USAAF bombers sank her for good on 23 October 1943.

Cattaro (former Yugoslavian *Dalmacija*): An old protected cruiser launched on 1899, *Cattaro* was immobilized at Pola for lack of fuel. The Germans captured her intact and commissioned her as *Niobe* on 8 November 1943. She stranded on 19 December 1943 on the Dalmatian island of Silba where the British motor torpedo boats *MTB276* and *298* sank her three days later.

Destroyers

Sebenico: Undergoing major refit in Venice. The Germans captured and commissioned her on 17 October 1944 as *TA43*. They scuttled her at Trieste on 1 May 1945.

Pigafetta: Undergoing major refit in Fiume from 28 June 1943. Her crew sabotaged her, but the Germans commissioned her as *TA44* on 14 October 1944. RAF bombers sank her on at Trieste 17 February 1945.

Dardo: Repairing at Genoa after suffering a machinery defect on 23 July 1943. She was scheduled to be operational by 1944. The Germans commissioned her as *TA31* on 17 June 1944, but due to machinery problems she was paid off on 20 October 1944 and scuttled on 24 April 1945.

Maestrale: Repairing at Genoa after being mined on 9 January 1943 and scheduled to be operational by late spring 1944. The Germans cannibalized her for spare parts and she was scuttled on 24 April 1945.

Premuda: She was scheduled to complete repairs at Genoa by early 1944 after suffering a severe machinery breakdown on 17 July 1943. The Germans commissioned her as *TA32* on 18 August 1944. She was scuttled on 24 April 1945.

Corazziere: Under repair at Genoa after colliding with a German landing craft on 5 February 1943 and being further damaged in a USAAF raid over Naples on 15 February 1943; not scheduled to be operational until summer 1944. The Germans cannibalized her for spare parts and she was sunk in an USAAF raid on 4 September 1944.

FR21 (ex French destroyer *Lion*): Under repair at La Spezia after suffering a machinery defect in early September 1943. She was scuttled on 9 September. The Germans considered her not worth salvaging.

FR 22 (ex French destroyer *Panthère*): Under repair for machinery defects at La Spezia since early September 1943. She was scuttled on 9 September. The Germans considered her not worth salvaging.

Zeno: Under repair at La Spezia after a 28 February 1943 collision with her sister ship *Da Noli* with completion scheduled for spring 1944. She was scuttled on 9 September. The Germans considered her not worth salvaging.

Torpedo boats

Dezza: Under minor refit at Fiume since late August 1943. Captured and commissioned on 9 June 1944 by the Germans as *TA35*. She was mined and sunk on an old Italian barrage off Pola on 17 August 1944.

Impavido: She was laying at La Spezia with boiler defects, but managed to sail to Portoferraio where she remained immobilized. The Germans seized her when the island surrendered on 17 September. They commissioned her on 9 October 1943 as *TA1*, but modified the name that month to *TA23*. She struck an Italian mine off Capraia Island on 25 April 1944 and was subsequently scuttled.

Lira: Under refit at La Spezia and scuttled there on 9 September but only minor flooding resulted. In March 1944 the Germans decided to commission her as *TA49*. Her repairs were still underway when she was bombed and sunk in a USAAF raid on Spezia on 4 November 1944.

Procione: Immobilized at La Spezia with machinery defects and scuttled on 9 September.

Ghibli: Immobilized at La Spezia by a boiler defect and scuttled on 9 September. The Germans raised and towed her to Genoa. In October 1943 she was scheduled to be consigned to the RSI navy, but was never repaired and was scuttled again on 24 April 1945.

Cascino: Under refit at La Spezia where she was scuttled on 9 September.

Montanari: Under repair at La Spezia after being bombed in an 8 February 1943 USAAF raid on Naples. She was scuttled on 9 September, raised by the Germans and sunk on 4 October 1944 in an Allied air raid.

Papa: Under refit at La Spezia. She was commissioned by the Kriegsmarine as *SG20* on 17 October 1943; however, the Germans paid her off on 1 November 1943 after overloading her with mines, causing the hull to collapse. She was scuttled on 24 April 1945 at Oneglia.

Partenope and *La Masa* were both refitting at Naples. The Germans sabotaged them at the end of September when they evacuated the city and they were never repaired.

Corvettes

Persefone: Repairing machinery defects at La Spezia. The Germans commissioned her as *UJ2227* on 2 December 1944; she was scuttled at Genoa on 24 April 1945.

Euterpe: Repairing machinery defects at La Spezia. The Germans commissioned her as *UJ2228* on 15 October 1944; she was scuttled on 24 April 1945 at Genoa.

FR51 (ex French *La Batailleuse*): Refitting at La Spezia and scuttled there on 9 September. The Germans raised and renamed her *SG23*, then assigned her in October 1943 to the RSI navy. They transferred her to Genoa for repair and in February 1945 designated her as *UJ2231*. However, she never commissioned and was scuttled at Genoa on 24 April 1945.

Antilope: Under repair at Leghorn after being damaged in an USAAF raid against that city on 28 May 1943 with completion scheduled for March 1944. The Germans commissioned her as *UJ6082* in 1944. The destroyer USS *Somers* sank her on 15 August 1944 in an action off the French Riviera.

Camoscio: At Leghorn repairing damage inflicted by USAAF fighter bombers off Sant'Agata on 24 July 1943. The Germans commissioned her as *UJ6081* in 1944. The destroyer USS *Endicott* sank her on 17 August 1944 in a surface action off the French Riviera.

Artemide: At Leghorn repairing damage suffered after being mined on 21 February 1943 with completion scheduled for March 1944. The Germans commissioned her as *UJ2226* on 12 July 1944 and scuttled her at Genoa on 24 April 1945.

Submarines

Otaria, Pisani, Settimo, Ametista and *Serpente*: These boats were assigned to the Pola and Fiume submarine and anti-submarine warfare schools. The first three sailed for Taranto while the last two scuttled off Ancona on 12 September.

Manara: Laying inoperative at Brindisi with a machinery defect.

Argo: Refitting at Monfalcone and sabotaged on 10 September. The Germans assigned her to the RSI navy, but she was sunk in an USAAF raid on 20 May 1944 before recommissioning.

Beilul: Refitting at Monfalcone. Captured and assigned to the RSI navy, she was sunk in an USAAF raid on 25 May 1944 just before recommissioning.

Nautilo: Fitting out at Monfalcone. She sailed to Venice on 9 September and was taken over by the Germans when the city surrendered. Transferred to Pola for completion, she was sunk there in a USAAF raid on 9 January 1944.

Ambra: At La Spezia repairing damage suffered on 18 July 1943 in an attack by Allied aircraft off Sicily. She was scuttled on 9 September and not considered worth salvage.

Bajamonti: At La Spezia for maintenance, she was scuttled on 9 September and not considered worth salvage.

Murena, *Sparide* and *Grongo* were fitting out at La Spezia to be used as attack craft carriers. They were scuttled on 9 September. All were raised and sent to Genoa. *Sparide* and *Grongo* were destroyed there in an USAAF raid on 4 September 1944 when they were almost ready. *Murena* was seriously damaged on 2 September 1944 and never completed repairs.

Sirena and *Volframio*: Under refit at La Spezia and scuttled there on 9 September. The Germans raised and cannibalized them for parts.

Aradam: Under refit at Genoa where the Germans captured and delivered her to the RSI navy as an attack craft carrier. Seized by the Germans on 18 August 1944 and sunk by an USAAF bomber raid on 4 September 1944 just before commissioning.

The old cruiser *Bari*, the torpedo boat *Antares* and the corvette *FR52* (ex French *Commandant Rivière*) were all sunk in shallow waters at Leghorn in May and June 1943 by USAAF bombers. Their recovery was planned, but had not yet begun. The Germans raised *FR52* on January 1944 and planned to commission her as *SG22*, but she was never repaired. The destroyer *Freccia*, sunk on 8 August 1943 at Genoa by a RAF raid, was also slated for recovery, but the Germans rejected the program.

Ships building or not yet commissioned by the Regia Marina

Carriers

Aquila: Her conversion begun on July 1941 at Genoa, but work halted on June 1943 to give priority to torpedo boats, corvettes and smaller craft. On 31 August 1943 she was scheduled to be completed by spring 1944. The Germans partially dismantled her to recover 20-mm guns and strategic material. USAAF fighter-bombers slightly damaged her on 16 June 1944. *Aquila* was recovered floating on 28 April 1945. Although the Italian navy studied plans from 1945–1948 to complete her as an auxiliary vessel, she was finally broken up.

Sparviero: Conversion at Genoa begun on October 1942 and stopped on April 1943 just after she had been razed. The Germans expended the hulk as a block ship on 6 October 1944.

Figure 39. Genoa, 23 August 1943. The carrier *Aquila* was sitting nearly completed, but with work stopped since June 1943 due to more pressing needs for other types of smaller warships (Aldo Fraccaroli)

Battleships

Impero: Launched on 15 November 1939 at Genoa and building at Trieste. Work halted on April 1943 to give precedence to *Cavour*. On 31 August 1943 *Impero* was scheduled to be combat ready by spring 1945. The Germans partially dismantled her during winter 1943/1944 to salvage strategic materials. In January

1944 they used her as a target during the "Mistel project" drone bomb trials and finally scuttled the hull on 1 May 1945.

Cruisers

Etna and *Vesuvio*: Under construction at Trieste, but work had stopped in April 1943. The Germans salvaged some material and then abandoned the two hulls which were later formally included in the RSI navy list. They were towed in early January 1944 to Zaule Bay near Trieste and scuttled there on 1 May 1945.

FR11 and *FR12*: Former French ships *Jean de Vienne* and *La Galissonière* scuttled at Toulon 27 November 1942. They had been raised and were scheduled to be towed to Italy by mid-September 1943 and commissioned in 1945. The USAAF sank them on 24 November 1943 and 1 April 1944 respectively.

Mario: Work was halted and the hull used as oil depot at La Spezia with no plans to complete construction. Scuttled by the Germans in April 1945.

Figure 40. The cruiser *Augusto* at Ancona in November 1944 a year after being sunk in a USAAF raid (Erminino Bagnasco)

Silla: Construction halted and used as oil depot at Genoa with no plans for completion. Damaged in an USAAF raid on July 1944 and scuttled by the Germans in April 1945.

Germanico: Building at Castellamare di Stabia, and used as a floating battery. Her construction was halted in 1943 when 94 percent complete to give precedence to escorts. According to the late August 1943 schedule she was to be commissioned by early spring 1944. The Germans scuttled her on 28 September during their retreat from Naples. The Italian navy salvaged her postwar and she completed in 1956 as *San Marco*.

Augusto: Building at Ancona 95 percent complete. Sunk in an USAAF raid on 1 November 1943.

Destroyers

Spalato: Building at Spalato (Split). Her completion was scheduled for late 1944. She was abandoned by the Germans and scuttled in October 1944. Taken over by Yugoslavia and commissioned as *Split* in 1958.

Comandante Botti and *Comandante Ruta*: Building at Trieste. Their completion was scheduled for June 1945. The Germans cannibalized them for materials.

Comandante Casana, Comandante dell'Anno: Building at Ancona. Their completion was scheduled for December 1944. The Germans cannibalized them for materials and wrecked the hulls before their retreat in July 1944.

Corsaro (ex *Squadrista*): Building at Leghorn and scheduled for completion in October 1943. In November 1943 the Germans towed her to Genoa. The decision to use her as a night fighter direction ship delayed progress and USAAF bombers sank her on 4 September 1944 just before completion.

Carrista: Building at Leghorn. Broken up by the Germans during autumn 1943.

Figure 41. Leghorn May 1943. The destroyer *Carrista* still on the slip with much work to be done. (Aldo Fraccaroli)

FR24 (ex French *Valmy*): The Germans towed her to Genoa from Savona and discarded her there.

FR32 (ex French *Le Siroco* ex *Le Corsaire*): Repairing at Genoa and scheduled for commissioning in 1944. The Germans halted work and scuttled her as a blockship on 28 October 1944.

FR33 (ex French *L'Adroit*, ex *L'Epée*): At Toulon. Scheduled to be towed to Genoa to be broken up there to provide spare parts for her sister ships.

FR34 (ex French *Lanquenet*): At Imperia waiting to be towed to Genoa to be repaired there during 1944. In June 1944 the Germans decided to commission the ship as *TA34*. She was scuttled still uncompleted on 24 April 1945.

FR35 (ex French *Le Bison* ex *Le Filibustier*): At Toulon waiting to be towed to Genoa to be completed during 1944.

FR36 (ex French *Le Foudroyant* ex *Fleuret*): waiting to be towed to Genoa to be repaired during 1944.

FR37 (ex French *Le Hardi*): At Savona waiting to be towed to Genoa to be repaired there during 1944/45.

The modern French destroyers *Mameluck* and *Casque* of the same class, still recovering at Toulon on 8 September 1943, were scheduled for transfer to Genoa in 1944/45. They had not received an Italian name.

Comandante De Cristofaro, Comandante Toscano at Riva Trigoso and *Comandante Margottini, Comandante Baroni* and *Comandante Borsini* at Leghorn were scheduled to be completed between December 1944 and June 1945. The Germans stripped and abandoned them. A September 1945 program to complete the two ships at Riva Trigoso was cancelled in 1946 due to concerns about being required to hand them over under the pending peace treaty. Some of their material was used in 1950 for the first two new Italian navy destroyers, *Indomito* and *Impetuoso*.

Torpedo boats

Gladio, Spada, Daga, Pugnale, Lancia, Alabarda: Building at Trieste with completion scheduled between October 1943 and January 1944. The Germans completed them as:

TA37: 8 January 1944. Sunk 7 October 1944 in the Aegean Sea by the British destroyers *Termagant* and *Tuscan*.

TA38: 12 February 1944. Scuttled in the Aegean on 13 October 1944.

TA39: 27 March 1944. Mined in the Aegean on 16 October 1944.

TA40: 17 October 1944. Damaged by USAAF bombers on 20 February 1945 at Trieste and scuttled there on 1 May 1945.

TA41: 7 September 1944. Damaged by British bombers on 17 February 1945 at Trieste and scuttled at Muggia on 1 May 1945.

TA42: 30 January 1945. Sunk by USAAF bombers at Venice on 21 March 1945.

Stella Polare, Spica, Fionda and *Balestra*: These ships were building at Fiume and scheduled for completion between October 1943 and March 1944. Taken over by Germany as *TA36, TA45, TA46* and *TA47*. The only two to complete were:

TA36: 13 January 1944. Mined off Fiume on an Italian field, 18 March 1944.

TA45: 6 September 1944. Sunk 13 April 1945 by British MTBs off the Istria peninsula.

The other two passed to the Yugoslavian navy in 1948 and *Balestra* completed as *Ucka* in 1949.

Intrepido, Arturo, Auriga, Rigel, Eridano, Dragone: Fitting out at Genoa and scheduled for commissioning or completion in 1943. They entered German service as:

TA25: 16 January 1944. USN PT boats sank her off La Spezia on 15 June 1944.

TA24: 4 October 1943. The British destroyers *Meteor* and *Lookout* sank her off Corsica on 18 March 1945.

Figure 42. *TA24* ex *Arturo*. She entered service under the German flag quickly and with little modification and provided a year and a half of hard service with the Kreigsmarine's 10th Torpedoboat Flotilla. (STORIA militare)

TA27: 28 December 1943. USAAF bombers sank her on 9 June 1944 at Portoferraio.

TA28: 27 February 1944. USAAF bombers sank her at Genoa 4 September 1944.

TA29: 27 February 1944. The British destroyers *Meteor* and *Lookout* sank her off Corsica on 18 March 1945.

TA30: 27 March 1944. USN PTs sank her off La Spezia 15 June 1944.

Corvettes

Colubrina, Spingarda, Carabina, Bombarda, Scure, Clava and *Zagaglia*: Building at Porto Marghera (Venice) and scheduled to complete between October 1943 and September 1944. Taken over by the Germans as:

UJ205: 1 January 1944. Sunk by USAAF bombers at Sebenico on 27 March 1944.

UJ206: Never commissioned. Damaged in a USAAF raid on 4 April 1944. Scuttled 26 April 1945; recovered by the Italian Navy in 1945 and completed in 1951.

UJ207: Never commissioned. Damaged in an USAAF raid on 4 April 1944. Scuttled on 26 April 1945.

UJ208: 22 April 1944. Sunk by the British destroyers *Avon Vale* and *Wheatland* on 1 November 1944 off Pag Island in the Adriatic.

The others, *UJ209*, *UJ210* and *UJ211* were never commissioned after being damaged in a 1 May 1944 air raid.

Egeria, Melpomene, Tersicore and *Euridice*: Building at Monfalcone and scheduled for completion between October 1943 and December 1943. Taken over by the Germans as:

UJ201: 28 January 1944. Sunk by the French destroyers *Le Terribile* and *Le Malin* on 28 February 1944 off Premuda Island in the Adriatic.

UJ202: 24 April 1944. Sunk by the British destroyers *Avon Vale* and *Wheatland* on 1 November 1944 off Pag Island.

UJ203: Damaged by USAAF bombers on 20 April 1944 and never commissioned; scuttled on 1 May 1945.

UJ204: May 1944; damaged by USAAF bombers on 25 May 1944 and scuttled on 1 May 1945.

FR53, FR54 and *FR55* (former French *Chamois, L'Impétueuse* and *La Curieuse*): Refitting at Toulon and planned for completion by the end of 1943. The Germans captured and renamed them *SG18, SG17* and *SG16*. The first commissioned on May 1944 and scuttled at Marseille on 22 August 1944; the other two were damaged by USAAF bombers on 24 November 1943 and never repaired.

Tuffetto: At Genoa nearing completion. She commissioned as *UJ2222* on 20 February 1944 but was damaged by USN PTs off Corsica on 24 May 1944; further damaged by USAAF bombers at Genoa on 4 September 1944 and scuttled there on 24 April 1945.

Marangone: At Genoa nearing completion. Commissioned as *UJ2223* on 18 March 1944 and sunk by USN PTs on 24 May 1944.

Strolaga: At Genoa nearing completion. Commissioned as *UJ2224* on 18 April 1944; damaged by USAAF bombers at Genoa on 4 September 1944 and lost four days later.

Ardea: At Genoa nearing completion. The Germans took her as *UJ2225* but never completed work and finally scuttled her at Genoa on 24 April 1945.

Capriolo: At Leghorn nearing completion. Commissioned as *UJ6083* (later *UJ2230*) in 1944 and sunk on 4 September 1944 during an USAAF raid over Genoa.

Alce: At Leghorn nearing completion. Commissioned as *UJ6084* in 1945 and scuttled at Genoa on 24 April 1945.

Renna, Daino, Cervo, Stambecco: Building at Leghorn and scheduled for completion by June 1944. Named by the Germans respectively *UJ6085, UJ6086, UJ6087* and *UJ6088* but all were damaged in an USAAF raid on 4 September 1944 and never completed.

Lucciola, Libellula, Grillo, Cicala, Calabrone, Cavalletta, Crisalide and *Farfalla*: Building at Castellammare di Stabia and scheduled for completion between October 1943 and September 1944. The Germans scuttled or sabotaged all eight on 17 September 1943. The Italian navy commissioned *Crisalide* and *Farfalla* in 1952 and 1953 respectively.

Figure 43. The corvette *UJ2225* ex *Ardea* January 1944. Although in an advance state of construction when captured, the Germans never completed her. (Erminio Bagnasco)

Submarines

R7, R8, R9, Bario, Litio, Sodio, Potassio, Rame, Ferro, Piombo, Zinco, Cromo, Ottone, Cadmio, Vanadio, Iridio, Rutenio, Oro: Building at Monfalcone and scheduled for completion between November 1943 and October 1944. The first twelve were taken over by the Germans as *U-It4, U-It5, U-It6, U-It7, U-It8, U-It9, U-It10, U-It11, U-It12, U-It13,* and *U-It14*. None were completed. *Bario* completed in 1961 as *Pietro Calvi*.

Dandolo: Under refit at Taranto.

Mameli, Da Procida and *Speri*: Being modernized at Taranto since December 1942. Work completed in 1944.

R3, R4, R5, R6, Magnesio, Mercurio and *Amianto*: Building at Taranto and scheduled to be completed for trials and training between December 1943 and October 1944. Work was halted by Allied order on September 1943.

FR112 (former French *Saphir*): At Naples. Not operational. Used from 21 April 1943 as a pontoon to charge submarines batteries. Scuttled by the Germans in September 1943.

FR115 (former French *Dauphin*): At Pozzuoli. Put in reserve in February 1943 for lack of spares. Scuttled by the Germans on 15 September 1943.

FR114 (former French *Espadon*): At Castellammare di Stabia. Put in reserve on February 1943 for lack of spares. Scuttled by the Germans on 13 September 1943.

FR113 (former French *Requin*): At Genoa. Put in reserve on February 1943 for lack of spares.

Poincaré: Just arrived in Genoa from France. The probable Italian name would have been *FR118*.

R10, *R11*, *R12*, *Alluminio*, *Antimonio*, *Fosforo*, *Manganese*, *Zolfo* and *Silicio*: Building at La Spezia. They were scheduled to be completed and ready for trials between December 1943 and December 1944. The Germans renamed the first three *U-It1*, *U-It2* and *U-It3*. None completed and work was suspended by March 1944.

On 31 August 1943 the Italian naval programs for 1944 and 1945 specified the construction of the following warships:

Eleven destroyers of the Comandanti class.

Eighteen torpedo boats of the *Ariete* class.

Two corvettes.

Twelve submarines of the *Tritone* class.

None were laid down or even named before the armistice although about one third of the necessary steel had already been supplied to the yards. Acquisition of other necessary material like copper, tin, bronze and brass was becoming increasingly difficult.

APPENDIX IV. THE POSTWAR DISPOSITION OF THE FLEET

Although the de Courten-Cunningham accord specified that no Italian warships other than those seized from the Allies would be surrendered, the British and Soviet governments insisted on the execution of the "long terms" and Badoglio, against his will and trusting in the ultimate good intentions of the Allies, signed this document at Malta on 29 September 1943. Badoglio then implored De Courten to amend his previous agreement with Cunningham that would allow the Allies to claim Italian warships. De Courten reluctantly did this on 17 November 1943 trading his signature for the deletion, by the Allies, of the words "Unconditional Surrender" from the armistice text.[89]

Between 1949 and 1951 Italy delivered the following major warships as war reparations to:

France: the cruisers *Attilio Regolo* and *Scipione Africano*; the destroyers *Oriani*, *Legionario*, *Mitragliere* and *Velite*; and the sloop *Eritrea*.

Greece: the cruiser *Eugenio di Savoia*.

USSR: the battleship *Cesare*; the cruiser *Duca d'Aosta*; the destroyers *Artigliere* and *Fuciliere*; the torpedo boats *Animoso*, *Ardimentoso*, *Fortunale*; and two submarines.

Yugoslavia: torpedo boats *Aliseo*, *Indomito*, *Ariete*.

In addition, the battleships *Italia* and *Vittorio Veneto* were assigned to the United States and the United Kingdom, but were refused and ended up being scrapped in Italy. Meantime the U.S. Navy gave Italy two destroyers, three destroyer escorts, three ex-German fleet minesweepers and two submarines, and promised a light carrier and an escort carrier. Considering the fact that most the surrendered Italian ships were worn out, or wartime constructions, it was not a bad bargain, even if objections by the Italian air force scuttled the delivery of the carriers.

---

[89] De Courten, *Le memorie*, 367-375. Fioravanzo, *La Marina dall'8 settembre alla fine del conflitto*, 101-110.

BIBLIOGRAPHY

Acerbo, Giacomo. *Tra due plotoni d'esecuzione*. Bologna: Cappelli Editore, 1968.

Agarossi, Elena. *A Nation Collapses: The Italian Surrender of September 1943*. Cambridge: Cambridge University Press, 2000.

Alegi, Gregory. "L'ala infranta," *Storia Militare* 100, (January, 2002): 15-21.

Amici, Andrea. *Un pomeriggio di settembre*. Genoa: De Ferrari, 2006.

Badoglio, Pietro. *Italy in the Second World War*. Westport Conn.: Greenwood Press, 1976.

Bagnasco, Erminio. *Corsari in Adriatico 8-13 settembre 1943*. Milan: Mursia, 2006.

---. *In guerra Sul Mare: Navi e marinai italiani nel secondo conflitto mondiale*. Parma: Ermanno Albertelli, 2005.

Bagnasco, Erminio and Enrico Cernuschi. *Le Navi da Guerra italiane 1940-1945*. Parma: Ermanno Albertelli, 2003.

Barca, Luciano. *Buscando per mare con la Decima Mas*. Rimini: Editori Riuniti, 2001.

Bargoni, Franco. *Esploratori, fregate, avvisi e corvette*. Rome: Ufficio Storico della Marina Militare, 1974.

Benigno, Jo di. *Occasioni mancate*. Rome: S.E.I., 1945.

Bernardi, Giuseppe. *La Marina, gli armistizi e il trattato di pace*. Rome: Ufficio Storico della Marina Militare, 1979.

Bolla, Luigi. *Perchè a Salò*. Milan: Bompiani, 1982.

Botti, Ferruccio "L'8 Settembre 1943 sulla corazzata *Giulio Cesare*," *Storia Militare* 3, (December 1993): 7-14.

Bragadin, Marc' Antonio. *The Italian Navy in World War II*. Annapolis: Naval Institute, 1957.

Bucciante, Giuseppe. *I generali della dittatura*. Milan: Mondadori, 1987.

Butcher, Harry C. *My Three Years with Eisenhower: The Personal Diary of Captain Harry C. Butcher, USNR Naval Aide to General Eisenhower, 1942 to 1945*. New York: Simon and Schuster, 1946.

Canevari, Emilio. *La guerra italiana*. Rome: Tosi, 1949.

Canosa, Romano. *Storia dell'epurazione in Italia*. Milan: Baldini e Castoldi, 1999.

Cardea, Mario. "La brillante azione della Torpediniera *Aliseo*," *Mare* (September 1952): 1-4.

Castellano, Giuseppe. *La guerra continua*. Milan: Rizzoli, 1963.

Cervone, Pier Paolo. *Caviglia, l'anti Badoglio*. Milan: Mursia, 1997.

Churchill, Winston S. *The Hinge of Fate*. Boston: Houghton Mifflin Company, 1950.

Cunningham, Andrew Browne. *A Sailor's Odyssey*. London: Hutchinson, 1951.

Da Zara, Alberto. *Pelle d'ammiraglio*. Verona: Mondadori, 1949.

Deakin, F.W. *The Brutal Friendship: Mussolini, Hitler and the Fall of Italian Fascism*. New York: Harper & Row, 1962.

Dear, I. C. B., ed. *The Oxford Companion to World War II*. New York: Oxford University Press, 1995.

De Courten, Raffaele. *Le memorie dell'ammiraglio De Courten*. Rome: Ufficio Storico della Marina Militare, 1993.

De Felice, Renzo. *Mussolini l'alleato*. Turin: Einaudi, 1997.

del Minio, Giuseppe. "Memorie di un comandante di cacciatorpediniere," *Il mare* (June 1959).

D'Este, Carlo. *World War II in the Mediterranean: 1942–1945*. Chapel Hill, N.C.: Algonquin Books, 1990.

Dondoli, Alessandro. "Piombino, settembre 1943," *Storia Militare* 72, (September 1999): 4-14.

Faldella, Emilio. "La resistenza degli italiani all'Elba," *Storia Illustrata* 190, (September 1973): 8-9.

---. *L'Italia e la seconda guerra mondiale*. Bologna: Cappelli, 1960.

Ferrucci, Ferruccio. *Kriegsgefangener 1943*. Ferrara: Cartografica, 2003.

Fest, Joachim. *Staatsreich, Der lange Weg zum 20 Juli*. Berlin: Wolf Jobst Siedler Verlag, 1994.

Festorazzi, Roberto. *Farinacci, l'antiduce*. Rome: Il Minotauro, 2004.

Fioravanzo, Giuseppe. *La Marina dall'8 settembre 1943 alla fine del conflitto*. Rome: Ufficio Storico della Marina Militare, 1971.

---. *La Marina nella Guerra di Liberazione e nella Resistenza*. Rome: Ufficio Storico della Marina Militare, 1995.

Fontana, Lapo Mazza. *Italia über alles*. Milan: Boroli Editore, 2006.

Fortuna, Piero. "Quella notte al Brennero," *Storia Illustrata* 310, (September 1983): 51-53.

Franconi, Giorgio. "Una corvetta della Regia Marina attraverso l'armistizio," *Storia Militare* 58, (July 1998): 51-60.

Franzinelli, Mimmo. *Guerra di spie*. Milan: Mondadori, 2004.

Freivogel, Zvonimir. "Siluranti ex italiane sotto bandiera tedesca," *Storia Militare* 36, (September 1996): 18–29; and 37, (October 1996): 22–35.

Eisenhower, Dwight. *Crusade in Europe*. Garden City, N.Y.: Doubleday, 1948.

Galbiati, Enzo. *Il 25 luglio e la MVSN*. Milan: Bernabò, 1950.

Galuppini, Gino. "L'Arsenale di La Spezia nel centenario della sua inaugurazione," *Rivista Marittima* (July 1969): 7-22.

---. "Il discorso dell'ammiraglio Bergamini," *Bollettino d'Archivio dell'Ufficio Storico della Marina Militare* (June 1998): 97-110.

---. "Pennello nero, part one," *Storia Militare* 47, (August 1997): 4-12.

---. "Pennello nero, part two," *Storia Militare* 48, (September 1997): 45-53.

Garland, Albert N. and Howard McGaw Smyth. *Sicily and the Surrender of Italy*. Washington, D.C.: U.S. Government Printing Office, 1965.

Garofalo, Franco. *Pennello nero*. Rome: Edizioni della Bussola, 1946.

Greene, Jack and Alessandro Massignani. *The Black Prince and the Sea Devils: The Story of Valerio Borghese and the Elite Units of the Decima MAS.* Cambridge, Mass.: Da Capo, 2004.

Gonzaga, Arturo Catalano. *Per l'onore dei Savoia.* Milan: Mursia, 1996.

Guariglia, Raffaele. *Memorie.* Naples: Scientifiche Italiane, 1950.

Herde, Peter. "Il Giappone e la caduta di Mussolini. La fine del regime fascista agli occhi di "Magic." *Nuova Storia Contemporanea* (5/2000): 113-36.

Hinsley, F. H.. *British Intelligence in the Second World War: Abridged Version.* New York: Cambridge University Press, 1993.

Kesselring, Albert. *Kesselring: A Soldier's Record.* New York: William Morrow, 1954.

Krellenberg, Manfred. "L'affondamento dell' Elbano Gasperi," *Storia Militare* 68, (May 1999): 43-49.

Lamb, Richard. *The Ghosts of Peace 1935-1945.* Wilton, Salisbury: Michael Russel Publishing, LTD, 1987.

Leonardis, Massimo de. "Il generale Antonio Sorice Ministro della Guerra," *Nuova Storia Contemporanea* (2/2004): 37-48.

Levi, Aldo. *Avvenimenti in Egeo dopo l'armistizio.* Rome: Ufficio Storico della Marina Militare, 1972.

Longo, Gisella. "La presidenza di Camillo Pelizzi all'Istituto nazionale di cultura fascista (1940-1943)," *Storia Contemporanea* (December 1993): 901-948.

Lochner, Louis P., ed. *The Goebbels Diaries 1942-1943.* New York: Doubleday & Company, 1948.

Lombardi, Gabrio. *L'8 Settembre fuori d'Italia.* Milan: Mursia, 1967.

Marcon, Tullio. "Union Jack a mare!" *Aria alla rapida* (March 2004): 14-15.

Massimo, Filippini. *I caduti di Cefalonia: fine di un mito.* Rome: IBN, 2008.

Mattesini, Francesco, *La Marina e l'8 settembre,* ed. Ufficio Storico della Marina Militare, Roma, 2002

Mattioli, Marco. "Operazione Centro Marte," *Storia e Battaglie* 82, (June 2008): 13-24.

Maugeri, Franco. *From the Ashes of Disgrace*. New York: Reynal & Hitchcock, 1948.

McGaw Smyth, Howard. "The Armistice of Cassibile," *Military Affairs* 12(1), (Spring 1948): 12-35.

Monelli, Paolo. *Roma 1943*. Milan: Longanesi, 1963.

Morison, Samuel Eliot. *History of United States Naval Operations in World War II. Vol. IX, Sicily–Salerno–Anzio, January 1943–June 1944*. Boston: Little, Brown, 1990.

Mureddu, Matteo. *Il Quirinale del Re*. Milan: Feltrinelli, 1977.

Mussolini, Benito. *My Rise and Fall*. Cambridge, Mass.: Da Capo, 1998.

la Nasa, Marino. "Il pomeriggio in cui l'Alagi sfuggì ai tedeschi dopo la cattura," *Aria alla rapida* (15).

O'Hara, Vincent P. "Attack and Sink." *World War II* (March 2004): 44-48.

---. *Struggle for the Middle Sea: The Great Navies at War in the Mediterranean 1940-45*. Annapolis: Naval Institute Press, 2009.

Ortona, Egidio. *Diplomazia in guerra*. Bologna: Il Mulino, 1993.

Pardini, Giuseppe "Le ultime ore del PNF, il processo Scorza," *Nuova Storia Contemporanea* (6/2001): 65-100.

Pelagalli, Sergio. "L'8 settembre a Berlino," *Storia Militare* 7, (April 1994): 14-19.

Pirelli, Alberto. *Taccuini 1922/1943*. Bologna: Il Mulino, 1984.

Puntoni, Paolo. *Parla Vittorio Emanuele III*. Milan: Palazzi, 1958.

Rohwer, Jürgen and Gerhard Hümmelchen. *Chronology of the War at Sea 1939-1945*. Annapolis: Naval Institute Press, 2006.

Rogers, Anthony. *Churchill's Folly: Leros and the Aegean*. London: Cassell, 2003.

Roskill, Stephen. *The War at Sea Volume III: The Offensive Part 1*. London: HMSO, 1960.

Sandalli, Paolo. *8 settembre 1943: forze armate e disfattismo*. Rome: Gruppo Editoriale Gesualdi, 1993.

Schenk, Peter. *Kampf um die Ägäis*. Hamburg: E.S. Mittler & Sohn, 2000.

Schreiber, Gerhard. *I militari italiani internati nei campi di concentramento del Terzo Reich*. Rome: Ufficio Storico dello Stato maggiore dell'Esercito, 1992.

Segreto, Luciano. *Marte e Mercurio industria bellica e sviluppo economico in Italia 1861-1940*. Milan: Franco Angeli, 1997.

Simpson, Michael. *The Cunningham Papers. Vol. 2, The Triumph of Allied Sea Power 1942–1946*. Aldershot, England: Ashgate, 2006.

Taylor, Maxwell D. *Swords and Plowshares*. Cambridge, Mass.: Da Capo, 1990.

Trye, Rex. *Mussolini's Soldiers*. Osceola, Wisc.: Motorbooks International, 1995.

Ufficio Storico Stato Maggiore Esercito. *Saggi di Storia Etico-Militare*. Rome: 1976.

---. *Memorie storico Militar*. Rome: 1977.

United States Department of State / *Foreign relations of the United States. Conferences at Washington and Quebec, 1943*. Substantive Preparatory Papers, *The Chargé at Vatican City (Tittmann) to the Secretary of State*. http://digicoll.library.wisc.edu.

---. C.C.S 311 Enclosure, "Suggested Action on Italian Peace Feelers."

Varsori Antonio. "Italy, Britain and the Problem of a Separate Peace during the Second World War: 1940-1943." *The Journal of Italian History* (3/1978): 455-491.

Von Senger und Etterlin, Frido. *Neither Fear nor Hope*. New York: E. P. Dutton, 1964.

Vigna, Achille. *Aeronautica italiana, dieci anni di storia: 1943-1952*. Parma: Albertelli, 1997.

Zangrandi, Ruggero *L'Italia tradita*. Milan: Mursia, 1971.

Zanussi, Giacomo. *Guerra e catastrofe d'Italia*. Rome: Corso, 1946.

LaVergne, TN USA
27 November 2010
206300LV00004B